Poetry & Place
2015 Anthology

Edited by
Ashley Capes & Brooke Linford

Poetry & Place Anthology 2015
Copyright © 2016

Copyright of individual poems to respective authors.

Cover: www.indigoforest.weebly.com
Layout & Typset: Close-Up Books

All rights reserved. No part of this book may be reproduced in any form by any electronic or mechanical means including photocopying, recording, or information storage and retrieval without permission in writing from the authors.

ISBN-978-0-9945289-2-6

Published by Close-Up Books
Melbourne, Australia

Thanks to the poets who made all of this possible.

Local Positioning System

This corner is where the gutter backs up and the road floods.
It is dry now and everyone will forget until it rains again.

Keep going, up past where kittens popped out of the drain once, summer balls of fur and eyes, in front of the house where the piano teacher lived;

she said 'you have the hands of a flautist,' so the piano lessons didn't go far.
This line of trees was lopped around when I was in high school,

see how the branches have been cut to make a canyon for the power lines to pass through. It's all built up now: No. 32 is on the spot of the Paddock of One Sheep.

They've put a second storey on No. 29 and the hedge around No. 26 used to seem like something from a fairytale; things are taller when you are littler.

Turn right at the corner with the apartments. There was a girl who learned the violin, she lived in the one on the lower left. Mostly windows are blind eyes but at dusk

she'd put the light on, stage lighting her bowing. Exhibitionist. Maybe I was smarting from my piano teacher's words, but I see her ghost in the window every time I pass.

It's a long straight road next. In summer it is the best way to town because of the plane trees
The temperature drops 10 degrees instantly. And in autumn it rains itchy fluff

with the cockatoos up there ravaging the seed balls. No, that's not a cockatoo.
It's a scrap of paper in the wind.

Jane Downing

First Morning in Venice

How easy to lose one's point of origin,
the tourist at the next table reminds us.
Even once around the square
and you could be anyone anywhere,
one minute a temporary lagoon dweller
the next a misplaced fixture in time and space –
implausible spec in the eye of the camera.

She would be lost still, she claims,
were it not for the old man
who led her back ... eventually ...
through a succession of frescos,
across a fifteenth-century plaza,
somehow threading three floors
of hospital corridors
long ago inhabited by monks.

In one room they fixed his left leg,
in another his right eye, and there,
part of his heart. Returning him to life
time and again. *Miracolo*.

We listen like children intent on believing,
the walls of the hotel's breakfast room
closing in. We dismiss the guide map,
cold coffee and half-eaten pastries -
hungry for a tale of our own.

Outside: fabled alleys, web of waterways,
arched bridges, rumoured hauntings,
refugee history, the anonymity
of carnival masks - all waiting

to waylay us from whatever task,
whatever path it is we think we're on.

Jane Williams

Commit to Your City

Our mattress is bicoastal, our books
well traveled, all the dishes chipped.
The sofa is new, a commitment
to a bigger apartment, a lifestyle that affords
plants on sunny windowsills.
We see our new city through eyes
that have seen many cities, lived
in a few, sipped the water, sampled
the restaurants, survived the public
transportation, debated the merits
of parking lots and community pools.
Here, we see the bland light
of people passing one generation
to another, the same chance
at swing pushing and shop ownership.
We are confused by this,
attempt to acclimatize while mentally
arranging our apartment back
into a box, and writing down lists
of city names, wondering what
is strange there, what detail have we
forgotten about geography?

Caitlin Thomson

2015

What if I Knew of the Upstairs Lounge?

My feet were in the same sneakers
that squeaked the St. Francis gym floor,
when I first stepped off the sidewalk
of Chartres in August of '75,
crossed Iberville Street, near

the wooden stairwell where men
once climbed sixteen steps through
a steel door to a space where
the simple was spoken freely: *Did you
see that cute guy in the square? . . .
John's got a new boyfriend . . .
I told my sister last night . . .*
It was a lounge where men
found their own stories
in the faces mirrored there.

On long study breaks, walking
the Quarter, how many times
did I pass? I'll never know,
I never saw, I never let myself
dream there were steps I could climb
carrying stories like mine. But
what if I'd heard of the lounge,

how it ended on a June Sunday in '73
during pride on parade in cities
less Southern, less Catholic? The stairs
turned wind tunnel, an inferno ascended.
Sixteen minutes to extinguish
the fire and thirty-two lives. *What if*

I'd heard in my sixteenth summer

walking home after practice? The news
on my radio, its single earphone
and the tied strings of my sneakers
tangled in the sweat on my neck.
What if I'd heard? What if I knew

what followed the fire? Investigations
were half-hearted at best.
The newspapers cackled:
> *Bodies stacked*
> *like pancakes,*
> *mass of charred flesh,*
> *literally cooked--*

faggots like food, not people that mattered.

But what if I'd heard? Back when I twirled
a bottle of pills in my hands, quietly
drunk on the tile floor by the toilet,
after parties with friends who
didn't know me. Would hearing
have been enough water to douse
my doubts, make me swallow? *What if*

I'd heard all the jokes that rushed
through that city those days
in late June: Did you hear the one
about the flaming queens?
At first no church offered burial.
Instead the city's punch line:
bury them in fruit jars. What else
would you do in New Orleans back then
with the bodies of gay men?

But what if I'd heard before
my fire turned to ember? Would I have
marked the taut skin of my forehead
with their ashes, like a Lenten reminder
to let outrage flare into courage.

2015

I'm haunted
by what I might have become--
a young Phoenix, beautiful, fierce.

James Croteau

Domestic

Home as a haven. bolt hole. leave the world behind.
no longer a stray dog. unwrap layers of the real self.
palimpsest. onion. couch potato. a bit overcooked.
location of creativity. quirky alones. do research.
write novels. symphonies. build collections. too many
possessions. to protect. fill you up. clutter. now seen
as squalor. pathological home alone. too empty.
site of threat. sharehouse. narratives of grotty terrace
houses. sense of community. sex with improper strangers.
ideas & food stolen. home is the hunter. walking on
eggshells. headache from compromise. a house is not
a home.

home as a place of nostalgia. library as a home. art gallery.
museum. this feels like home. says client to psychotherapist.
faux home. surrogate mother. sheep may safely graze.
too expensive to maintain. marriage home. tete-a-tete. &
baby makes three. the kinderarchy. children rule. rosemary's
baby. we need to talk about kevin. tantrums. pester power.
some never leave home. merging generations. tolerance required.

neighbours. acoustic torture. arguments & vibrations. unwanted
tintinnabulations. the best neighbours invisible & inaudible.
renovations. facades in lieu of an inner life. new kitchens. paint
jobs. If you rent don't complain. no changes. upgrades. *a bird of
passage. my real home is elsewhere.*

old tvs radios. too obese. buy more. update to slimline. anorexic
objects. disappearing fast. but chairs & sofas for lounge lizards
become more corpulent. **my** bed. rumpled installation. tracey
emin. **without** sex drugs rock'n'roll.

2015

home as landscape of strangeness. *unheimlich*. zoom in. black umbrella drying in kitchen. vampire bat. shelters mourners at rain-sodden funerals. an ailing heart. broken ribs. dread reveals itself. *it is nothing & nowhere*. icicle. a transparent fish. Swims down the plughole.

Carolyn Gerrish

Dudgeon

do your neighbours know you write poems about them?
my friend asks as she sips her tea *nup!* my reply
above us ms thunder thighs does her dance exercise
boobs bobbing in *jesus loves me* t-shirt
she bangs on the floor *thumpbumpthump*s
measure time lost forever
or is this her god's displeasure in me down below?
my heart races jaw clenched shudder in the bones
while she extends her life is she ending mine?
t.a.b terry home from the club huffs and puffs
tops up with tinnies his *telly-vision* full blast
black and white celluloid chatter until 2am
downstairs deaf *mr stinky* reeks of urine
in an attempt to catch the clock
his radio wails a chorus of right wing overkill
next-door *doof-doof*'s electronic trance
agitates my heart rhythms into arrhythmia
to the beat of a bass track band
even the building walls contract and expand
understand the need for walls of sound
give illusion of solitude knee jerk reaction is let fly
tibetan monks chant *mantras for turbulent times*
instead cave in down low play stony ground's *alchemy*
throbthudthuds continue as background to seething rage
offer politely *more tea*?

Jenni Nixon

Woman Crying in the Supermarket

There's a woman crying
in the frozen food aisle
of the supermarket,
her tears are turning to ice on her cheeks,
her feet are encased in a pool of frozen tears.
She has one hand clutching her trolley
somewhere between the frozen peas
and the ice-cream compartments,
her other hand holds a mobile to her ear,
her mouth is slightly open.
People file past her, they look, stare,
they want her to move.
The aisle is slippery,
beginning to ice over with her frozen tears,
trolleys become stuck,
clogging the whole aisle,
even Security can't budge her.
Soon emergency workers arrive
with sharp tools and pressure hoses.
The ice is chipped and liquefied around her.
Lifted and placed in a trolley
like a tumbled statue
she is pushed through the fractured ice
away from the aisle,
past the fresh food section
where a man holding a ticket
and wearing a fish on his head
waits impatiently
for the deli to re-open.

Mark Miller

The Sea is Emptying

the sea smells stronger in the morning.
more things are drying as the stretched sun
reaches into jellyfish and dead sharks,
dragging them into the air.

feel their sting, i want to say, smell their bite!
but your eyes stroke the dog,
ploughing through the tide,
scattering salt water. he must be cold, you say
and feel his shivers.

i'm aware of them myself.
the beach is more an esplanade,
tracked against the cliff
with daily pilgrims passing,
seaweed slumped exhausted on the shells, gasping.
it seems the waves are frozen
till they crash against the shore and splinter.

still the wind, so strong a swimmer,
drifts to sea and sinks
as we find a place to settle round the point,
feet engrained in sand as grains of sand
seep into our shoes and up the cuffs of trousers.

each shell you hold looks
freshly minted; my hands are full of relics
that have given up their bodies,
sand to sand.

we stand, avoid an ambush
of dog dissolved in droplets,
and circling the head to face the south,

2015

we notice that the wind is gone,
like we were walking on the water
not the land.

Ben Walter

Undersong

If there is sky,
if there is summer,
if the sob through the pines has dulled
to a small wing's minor beat,
to a cricket's pulsing breath,
the day radiates the sibilance of eucalypt,
thin leaf edges turn to the sun.

And if rain veils the canopy,
weaves errant threads of timpani,
if sandstone drips staccato
and braided runnels lilt a rippled tone,
then the creek fattens,
sings soft arias.

We dare not move or speak,
hear undersongs we won't disturb,
believe we don't belong, think
all will vanish
like the puff of a fungus ball,
leaf shift, beetle click, seed split.

Shy ducklings rustle reeds,
our whispers peal like thunder.
We breathe too much.

Irene Wilkie

In the Lane Where I Live

in the lane where I live it slopes down, slopes South, to the West the poached egg of sun, and the lane has no lights, no kerbs, no paths but

has wild herbs, four types of rose and daubs of weed and the walls in the lane are made of stone, of brick and the one three up from us,

of wood, has been clipped and chopped and bashed and propped and in this lane the folk don't work, well not much, 'cept us and the one down from us

has two floors with lots of frills, all for two old folk with loads in the bank but far less in their days but they do speak to us, in

their patched up, pranged up tongue and the house at the end has no plants – no pots, no shrubs, no trees back or front while we live in a lush

plot of seeds and greens and blooms and dreams and we try to make sweet noise, try to make each a nice day, try to make a note to thumb

tack to our foreheads which says 'we're here, we're new and we'd like to like you', but I don't think the folk in the lane like blood or rhyme

Kevin Gillam

Brohmon (Journey)

ChaiChaiChaiChaiChaiChaiChai...
The old man's voice is a rusted bell, swinging
in time with the steel kettle he swings
like incense, summoning worshippers.
Salvation comes hot, cinnamon-spiced
in small clay cups.
– *Kitne?* I ask.
– *Four rupees,* he replies, a curled lip
and doubled price expressing his thoughts on my Hindi.
I will soon learn, not speaking English is an insult,
an assumption of poor education.
For now I pay up, sip the too-sweet tea. I keep on
sliding deeper into this sea where bodies, bobbing heads and
eyes and cries and even the screeching tyres, the never-silent
horns and motors speak
multiple tongues that have me licked.
– *Helloooo Mem...*
A young man tails me down the sarani.
– *You look my shop?*
– *Dhan'yabāda, Na.*
– *You speak Bangla, Mem?*
– *Chotto. I'm trying to learn.*
– *Why?*
Why indeed?
Everybody here speaks English,
albeit Indian English, queer
in its fastidiousness. The same fastidiousness
brought by colonists, along with cricket,
Victorian morality and trams.

In Australia, even England,
this language has been kicked about
like a stitched pig's bladder. It has stripped, streaked
across sunburnt fields, swum in murky dams,
surfed churning seas.
It has slept with strangers, tattooed names and numbers,
scars and smudges. It is wrinkled, wrung out, wrecked,
but still raging, still diving for each sweaty tackle,
each heaving throng.
Nobody ever called a white Australian savage
(though it frequently was and is apt).
Is this why India holds on to English – "proper" English, with such a firm
yet careful grasp?
– *Why you speak Bangla, Mem? Why?*
Lamp posts blossom bright with orange cardboard, bold letters:
LEARN ENGLISH NOW!
It's the only way to get a good job, any job
that's not lugging rickshaws.
The locals' want for language is a need, a palpable hollow, a hunger – literally.
My need is pure wanting, bourgeois fancy.
What are these new words, but souvenirs, pretty things
I see and want?
I flash my Namaskās like a shiny silver anklet, linguistic bling.
– *If you learn a language, Mem, learn Hindi.*
These Bengalis worship Kali. They don't even have a separate word for "drink".
They say, "I eat water." How stupid! All Bengalis are stupid.
Now, tell me, are you... experienced, Mem?
Mem?
I spin, eyeball the wannabe charmer in his denim jeans
and Nike cap.
– *Bakavāsa banda!* I spit.

The expletive socks him, stops him, mouth wide, looking hollow
like the drained clay cup I smash on the sidewalk, thinking this
is all the Hindi a white girl needs in such situations.
And so I continue, silent, en route to the Kali temple.

Amelia Walker

2015

The Home Midwife

She pulls up in a hatchback,
carries her leather case swollen
with years in and out of waters

a little vial of rose oil and herbs
transferred through bellyskin
to help the body yawn.

She walks down a hallway
to brew a pot of raspberry leaf,
fennel, stinging nettle

and chats between contractions,
makes a joke about stir frying the placenta
but doesn't laugh.

There's no phone code or knife sharpening
for spine on spine, head up bottom down
or umbilical wrapped around the neck

she has whispering hands;
chinese point massage to coach
an aquatic half somersault
and unfurl the ribbon.

She reads faces too
guides a father's hands
to be in on the magic of catching skin
slippery as water

it's a black art
to let a baby happen
in your living room.

Andrew Phillips

Mourning Morning

My mother's house surrounds
me in a shroud: the tinkling
of the teaspoon as my father stirs
his tea, his tea; the chug of the washing machine
that never dies. The tubular wind chimes casting
their cool auric spell around us; the complaint
of the floorboards bearing up our lives.
And the busyness, of the birds in bush nearby... I

lie with eyes shucked open, not turning
to what waits to be let in.
I hear the phone shriek—and again—
then footsteps up the hall; the sound
of hesitation at the door—
as I elongate this moment,
try to dwell inside before.

Michele Seminara

The Persistence of Memory

The Christmas box arrives and I stand over it eating M&M peanuts right out of the bag, shamelessly, pigging out because they're mine, American, and they taste like the fattening crowd, a dark Kmart parking lot, wet asphalt, tall lamplight, damp streets, sodden leaves, sweet autumn, sod, mulch, dirt, chain-link fence, concord grapes, early frost, cattails, Canada geese, corn stalks, Wisconsin River, Devil's Lake, deer hunt, tobacco sheds, white shirts, broad hats, the mule, a team of horses, Pa on the porch, Fireman's Park, baseball, grilled chicken, rhubarb, brush fires, train tracks, lightning storms, tornado sirens, mint farm, marsh grass, weeping willow, my mother's silver stapler, my father's tattoo, telephone wires, maple trees, the blue heron each morning I thought only I could see.

Rasma Haidri

Taj Mahal

Transit station, a camel market of coaches
disgorging pilgrims of love and architecture.
My ex-wife always wanted to come here,
a monument to undying love, she said.

The station is a mêlée – shouts, confusion,
centipedes of day trippers, couples holding hands.
If she was here alone she'd take a deep breath
and tolerate the crush. I have to stop this.

Armed soldiers with abrupt directional thumbs
and cocked trigger fingers check for guns and bombs
in the field of love. The search is brisk and thorough,
the atmosphere strangely calm, like a lawyer's office.

Red sandstone walls conceal the monument –
then, in a calculated square, quite suddenly,
four minarets, the dome and white façade –
love distilled. Abruptly, I can't breathe.

I want to stare at it, but stricken lovers
of photography have propped ahead of me
despite the crowd behind us pushing in –
so love becomes a crush, an eager, smiling

riot. To escape, I veer down steps
to a quiet Muslim garden where, my camera
still in its case, I find myself in middle years
derailed in a memorial to loss.

John Upton

Brisbane

I would like to write a love poem
for my city but it
is so ugly I think
brown river and sprawl
brown towers and breaking sun
But at night
when the river is just a sound
and the towers are floating lights
my city
I love you
You are hot and perfect
and on the ferry
   I bend my head to sleep

Jonathan Hadwen

Rozelle Window on Two Consecutive Days

1. Funny how

even the din of the neighbour
dismantling whitegoods in the street again
with a hammer and handaxe at six
in the evening can begin
to feel like home

2. Eventide

Look across
to those eucalypts
See them comb the currents
of the evening's freshening wind
Air is a fluid
and we all live beneath
its waves

Benjamin Dodds

Parallel to Shore

sacrificial leaves our tour guide unpacks nature for us just enough science so we're impressed how one species overcomes adversity *can you see them the yellowish leaves?* I look for my tube of sunblock too many cruises have left me burnt *mangroves store salt in nature's own throw-away packaging* I try every zip on my backpack *completely biodegradable* like me in the naked sun and now I've found it but missed a zoom on dying leaves and a wide on mud-swamp *total recycling* he doesn't use the word swamp of course he's perfected his language for us this is a *mangrove forest* I'm invader I work the white cream into my raw sacrificial skin careful not to leave a clown nose a baby next to me starts to laugh we all laugh it can't be my nose suddenly the guide pops the mic *look, there's a baby crocodile* the boat rocks on its hinges there must be three or four very young babies on this cruise nothing like the live numbers of mud crabs snacking on fresh yellow leaves *they store them in burrows* we don't see crabs in burrows I smile right along with the baby realising now what a clever auto-suggestion details of crabs in burrows we see them in our inner eye by the end of this cruise I will have "seen" hundreds of virtual mangrove animals actually two and a quarter crocodiles who enjoy only *a brief interlude for mating* all ears are pointed towards the twin speakers *the sex life of the crocodile* is crucial to the success of this cruise the sex life of crabs could also interest not sure about bacteria *crocodiles are cannibalistic and eat their own babies* at least they know what they are eating after this cruise I cramp up turn the colour of mud for two hours was it the thousand island dressing sweet chilli paste tartare sauce or the actual cruise-temperature prawns later I read of a rich ordinary diner poisoned death by asparagus sauce served with seafood we throw our head scraps to a rabbly school of river fish I throw off their name as soon as I hear it you can have too much of nature a day cruise

2015

has infinity to contemplate *a brahmeny kite* arrives as if on autocue skipper counts us off his lifejackets will outlive total depreciation we slip into land feet zap zap not mosquitoes just deleting a photo swarm of impressions   three average birds say twenty mangrove shots one blurred baby croc

Margaret Owen Ruckert

Reclining Tree

she
reclining across the Monaro
plains, limbs smooth, gleaming
odalisk, a single tree
exposed to merciless
raking wind and penetrating
sun
unruffled as an alabaster model
before the frisky brush of Renoir

all that the eye can see around
as we drive past her
is dry grass leaning south

this snow gum has found
her niche against the odds
nestled on the Monaro Plateau divan

Fiona McIlroy

An Afterlife of Stone

The lumpy wrinkled flesh
of some great ancient beast

a woolly mammoth
or elasmothere

lies mummified beside the Hume
near Gundagai.

She must have strayed here
so far south

on long-lost sunken land
or melted ice

and never found her way
back home.

Her body dried to rock
by endless sun and wind

spreads wide
across the plain.

Distant sheep are maggots
crawling on her lichened skin

their new-shorn fleece
the painful

almost-white of larvae
on raw meat.

Poetry & Place

She doesn't seem
to mind.

Perhaps the warm
quiet company

of woolly beasts
however small

still comforts her
in the long

slow afterlife
of stone.

Jenny Blackford

Field Church

Set back deep past rows of cotton stalks. Past bolls swollen with white foamy wisps and past bolls wet with rot. Set back against the pines and dogwoods and pecans that climb from the fields like cliffs before a green sea. The spire rises toward the clouds.

Whitewash peels from the shiplap planks. Window glass lies loose in mosaics of mud, brilliance, insect shells. Though inside, the pews are ordered, the pulpit upright, the wood stove massive with importance.

> in the muddy yard
> where the rain lilies tremble
> without a breeze

From the woods, we wander upon it, wander accidentally almost, while looking for the cemetery where the bluesman lay. We walk, for there is no road here, not much of a road, at least. Just an old loggers' gash. Rutted, smoky gray-black dirt when dry. When wet, mucky and thick, like the bottom of the river itself. The preacher we had met in town warned us of it in either state.

— No, you must walk.

— But which way?

— Walk by faith, not by sight, for His word is a lamp to your feet and a light to your path.

>   gray morning
>   possession vine slowly wraps
>   the rusted harrow

J. Todd Hawkins

Death in Nepal

Crossing a footbridge over the Bagmati River, I smell a queer smoke, and look inquiringly at Prem, our Gurkha guide, a Buddhist. "Hindu barbecue," he says, pointing. Bimal, our Kathmandu guide, wearing two red tikas from his morning worship, winces. Just below the bridge, on a simple wooden platform, a corpse shrouded in straw mats burns fitfully. Plumes of smoke rise as a barefoot man wearing only ragged shorts pushes small sticks of wood under the bier. I stare until I notice a cluster of grieving, wailing relatives, so I cross the bridge and climb higher on the grounds of Pashupatinath Temple to look without intruding. Another body, draped in an orange shroud mantled with marigolds, waits for burning. Beyond it are two more—one already laid out; the other, a bundle shrouded in pink, being dipped feet first into the river before being arranged on its bier. Cremations take place here because the Bagmati flows into the sacred Ganges. Downstream nearly naked children splash in the murky water. Surrounding the cremations crowds of people chat, sell firewood and straw, read newspapers, snack, beg, and flirt. Among them amble cows; above them, golden rhesus monkeys clamber over temple rooftops.

SuzAnne C. Cole

Thoughts from Above

Over Tel-Aviv, the stewardess pauses the film
and says *Fasten your seatbelts*.
I am looking out the window
searching for the coastline lights.
It's twelve after midnight, local time.
Memories from the land of my childhood and youth
are rising: orange orchards, citrus smelling winter,
a big family, a small village, the days before
the economic boom that replaced
our *Gemeinschaft* with *Gesellschaft* forever.

Film halts.

In the darkness I scan the scene:
Above stars hang and the waxing crescent
is gone. Below are little houses and tiny cars like fireflies
dancing in an urban forest.

Wheels pulled out, the pressure in the ears grows.

This time is different, this time I want to land,
to put my feet upon the yellowing lawns,
on the soft hot desert sand.
Everything is approaching, growing familiar
and threatening. A paradox only a land of birth
can contain. Preventing, enabling, wounding, yet secure.

The plane is mighty now, swooping down in the dark
toward the unknown. The first time I packed my life
and threw it over my back is ten years past
and long forgotten, it seems as if I was dreaming.

I've been infected by the wandering disease, I have

seen other landscapes, dipped my feet on other shores
and learned that on different mountains there are other answers for what is trivial and evil, I acquired new definitions of differences
and of the meaning of borders.

Pressure of descent pulls me back into reality, to this darkness
flying in the absence, pulls me back to my village and my home,
back to my soil. I have grazed in greener and cooler fields.
Can I see now with new eyes the blessings lying in this god's
plot which gave me everything and took away everything?

Mountain air is fresh as wine, Mount Zion fills my lungs
even inside the sailing iron skeleton. The waves carry lights
from the white city to break over its own shores.
Tel Aviv is ever awakening,
filling every corner possible and rising from the lowland
to the mountains of Jerusalem where Muhammad stormed up into the sky, where Jesus roasted in the sun and one man built (twice) the house of god. A modern symbol for everything lacking wit, love and god-fear. I shut my eyes and breathe in the city and its lights that I have so often hated, I breathe in the bible that stares at me from the sleeping hills to the east.

Landing.

Give me nature, earth,
let me feel the wind that plays among fruit trees and forests,
let me sleep with the *Shechinah*,
leave me alone with the morning's musical birds. Let the sun kiss me on my cheeks and bid me to wake up.

Guy Traiber

Tabula Rasa

1.   Time hangs around my place
like an errant friend who overstays, drives you mad
but then he leaves town & you grieve
for those moments of shambolic intimacy.

Can't be with him, maybe he's living in some community now
but I'm locked out of any gated communities,
still too young for retirement lifestyle villas,
too much of everything for lentils & the hippy drum.

Austerity breeds space,
space breeds foolishness which is precious.
Daniel smirks as I save the world. Ophelia says yes,
thinks loving is again possible.

There is no god, I will die.
Cultivate indifference
& a measured ethics that
even Cardinal Pell thinks will get us at heaven.

But I'm drunk again - with moment this week.
No one has been rescued.
The river's taxes spread the blame, my pains
like polite children fuster at my feet.

Above a colloquium of Pacific black ducks
I realise a jackhammer has been going on across the bay -
all morning. It is a small thing beside
remnant ideas & warming sun.

Mothers have rolled this day & are smoking it.
Hazard reduction is a universal goodity. Gilding the liver
we wear helmets to bed

our cloaks of haze are immortal.

This could (but won't) go on forever.
Local Rural Fire Service seems to have blended
a subtle mix of rum & feathers.
The secret is to peel a living from your skin.

2.   Back home around the poker table... Boredom
drinks your beer, has a take on everything.
A tottering Certainty is perennially bleak, he
needs a talking to.

Acceptance makes up the fourth, she's
already exhausted her stake
but has bet carefully & will go home
with small change in her pocket.

She lives in the past, but also in the present.
All our laughs come from her interjections.
That laughter is the real prayer
before this monstrance filled with bone dust.

Les Wicks

Don't Worry, I'll Go

I am going, somewhere
to Cyprus, where I belong
and I am sure you will be
relieved when I am gone

I am too loud for you anyway
& sometimes I honestly
can't be bothered climbing
your tall walls

fighting racism with racism
you started it
so we fought back
then you fought back
& we fought back
& now it's hard to recall
why it all began

It's not even your land anyway
but don't worry, I'll go
& I know you won't miss me
Maybe I'll miss you, sometimes
I might miss your coldness
as I walk along Cyprus'
endless Mediterranean blue
with golden heat enveloping me
on my way to the beach
on my lunch break
almost time for siesta

& I'll think

how stressed out you made me
for most of my life
How a group of Aussie boys
picked on me at primary school
& how mum and dad didn't
call it racism, just said
I had to learn to be strong

Yeah, I might think of you

sometimes

Koraly Dimitriadis

Fingal

It was much the same as any other
redneck town: more pubs
than happy marriages, a burdened
yet voiceless main road, at least one homo-
sexual without a choice.

Along its potholed highway, witchy
copses of gorse, always a carcass—
kangaroo, Major Mitchell, Devil—and willows
that wept their barbed and zealous roots
into the Esk.

Its men mined coal or raped
the conifers planted in pretty, crossed rows;
its women bitched and swapped
recipes for wild black swan and sickly-sweet jams
as freely as they swapped barbiturates;

its children, born with a stubbie of home-
brew in one hand,
a slug gun in the other, lazed
away the days like fattening pigs
in above-ground pools

riddled with the larvae of shiny black beetles
or in the oily glow from TV screens
that spread R-rated violence
and XXX sex rented from the wife-beater boar
at the video store.

Each day an inferno, Cerberus
picking the meat from my bones.
Each night magnifying, possessed

by at least one more falling
star than the last.

At thirteen, after a lifetime
of Christmases', Easters' and Sundays'
Black Masses, I unrolled the scrolls
of the Torah, swore to my psychotic father
a public and bloody suicide.

note: an earlier version was first published in Poetry Ireland Review, 2011

Stuart Barnes

Casglu Afalau / Apple Picking

i

The others tease.
Mary the Fifth, they call me.
Soon, I will be fifteen
and last year's boy returns to crush
the master's apples   for cider.

ii

It is not easy to keep yourself clean
Cook tells me
but you must try.
Her lips are thin as pastry.
Her eyes don't really trust me.

iii

Dust is my enemy.
The curtains betray me,
sending up a small cloud like an infant artillery.

iv

Best china for visitors. Ordinary cups today.
I'm running late.
The clock wags its pendulum, a stern finger.

Sir enters

and sits, pretends to remove some lint
from my skirt,
smoothes his palms on the thick fabric.

I curtsy and leave
his trembling hands,
his damp shillings.

    v

Everyone must be spared for apple picking.

Released from the kitchen's steam,
my cheeks turn red in the cold air.

I think of last year's boy,
the cider mill he travelled with.
I am fifteen and ready,
and the clouds seem to favour me
and the sun, too.

    vi

He works so hard, steam curls off him.
He looks away when he sees me
but looks back again quickly.

    vii

The costrels are waiting
to be carried out.
I carry one,
two, three easily
and the horn cups, too,
twice as many.

Under the biggest tree,
people are gathering.
I hand out cups that spill, sticky,
scent of apples all around me.

    viii

Finally, shyly, he comes to drink with me.
Our eyes meet over the brimming edges.

The taste of something stirs on our tongues.
Tart and sweet all at once.

Ivy Alvarez

Surface Tensions

The sunlight runs on wires in the vineyard
like the ghost of grapes
that have yet to be borne.

The hills are muscled in green pelts and amber
they slough their skins
with each shower of rain.

Snow gums wrestle with sharp winds and long
won't let their guard down
when the gales are gone.

The frosty moon waits for eclipse
while I breathe words at things
and watch them mist.

Duncan Richardson

Transience
(for Kim)

1 The Esplanade

round by the beach
        it's morning blue
                sunshine in your hand
like coloured pencils
      sanding light
            across a paper sky

2 Ocean Beach

Look at this lapis lazuli sea
and how you were girls in jeans
waiting on winter sand, waiting
for real talk to be lit
when the boys came out of the water.

They ran up the sand glittering,
flinging the sea and leg ropes,
their hands slipping fibreglass,
dumping boards deck down
or pegging tail and fin.

They peeled rubber suits away
from ice slivered muscles,
slipped flanny shirts over
cold salty skin, dried
in the telling of each wave.

They'd ask you girls for a light
and sometimes make a fire,

invisible, tossed to the wind

and winter sea, the stone
cold coastal rim.

3 Umina

At seventeen, you hung along
      the white surf club wall,
locals looking down the dune
      at holiday umbrellas.
From the top of the beach you only saw
      Hawaiian Tropic skin,
          your own world of summer
              borrowed from the islands:

coconut oil, puka shells,
      photo walls of Pipeline,
and Uluwatu stories, your
      brown bodies stranded
beneath the salt-fringed gaze
      of boyfriends who decreed
          Nothing will ever change –
              we'll bring our grandkids here!

Now, on a winter afternoon
      pale as a pink shell,
girls in hijabs stroll the sand,
      dogs and children leap
the tide, looking up the dune
      to safety fencing around
          construction of the new
              club at the top of the beach.

4 Booker Bay

on the marina wharf you
peered through the gaps
at water looping light around
sea splintered pylons,
rocking hulls and dreaming fish,
transient, exquisite,
like phosphorescent ocean stars
and your voyage out
leaping soundless from a surface
of dark deep water

Jill McKeowen

Canal Life

A tire bobbed like an oily cork
before being swallowed.
A school of supermarket carts
glinted like fish scales under
water thick with grease
as a colony of takeout cartons
mated on the shore.

Valentina Cano

My Inheritance

In my dreams I inhabit the paddocks
of my youth, broad expanses
of brown grass divided
by barbed-wire fences, scattered
with droppings and dung.

Riding on the monster tractor
with my grandfather
I revelled in the wind
drawing tears from my eyes.

I sucked in the smell
of the sheep and cows,
musty hay, molasses,
diesel and wheat.

I ran with the dogs,
chasing sheep
from where they grazed,
but they were only briefly disturbed,
soon settling down to fresh grass.

Between sunrise and bedtime
I lived an eternity, played
and worked, learnt and feasted.
My grandfather's land became my land.

His paddocks had been my father's
paddocks, and now they are mine.
In my mind the hot north wind

still flattens the brown grass
and carries the smell of sheep
and earth across the Pacific.

Nathanael O'Reilly

The Barn Roof

We could touch the sky on top of Kansas peaks.
The slope of silvery, slivery
peaks, gave feet and hands that seek
grips to scale the heights, quivering
muscles, weak, like a sparrow in grip
of barn owl, hiding in the loft
of barn rafters, tied in rope, a noose,
a swing to span bales of hay, we were Tarzan
in the dust motes, drifting in the light slices,
pouring from the maw of the barn. Mountain
climbers, birds perched, at the apex, set to fly
only in our dreams we could launch our bird
bodies skyward. Drifting in and out of hazy banks
of clouds. Freedom from words of ripped pants, frayed
shirts, and shingle pieces embedded in a child's skin.

Barbara A Meier

Sulfur

      it is possible for us
                                        at times unavoidable
            to live in a burning house
                          for years at a time
                  we will become desperate
                  of course
                to write on things
                        which survive flame
          a little better
at least
                        than paper
the first efforts will often be
                      ink on the end of needles
words pushed
        into the flesh
                  it becomes necessary
            eventually
                to carve
          into our own bones
                      and then whatever survives combustion
will be collected
     we'll call it history
          until the next fire

A. S. Patric

Solar Power

Half the houses
on that street
have solar power
but only one
has a cardboard sign
on the front lawn,

an advertisement
that buckles in the rain,
stapled onto
two scrawny
wooden posts,
looks as cheap
as a coupon
torn out of the paper.

The plastic is creased
like one of those
corrugated fences,
like you can see the
fold lines from when
it was scrunched up
in someone else's
pocket.

Half the houses
on that street
have solar power

but only one house

gets it discounted.

Karen Murphy

Monochromist

You're a poet; you must be
a patient man, he says, and offers

me a job. Having nothing better
to do except write poems, I take up

the brush and begin cutting in.
The house is big. Empty. Filled

with rooms without clear purpose.
Bland acres of dropcloths, carpet,

walls stretching 14 foot to ceilings:
vast polygons of cream. My bare

feet are paint-spattered and sure
of themselves, straddling the peak

of the ladder, the cocked brush
reifying the idea of a straight line,

framing the memories of tenants
so they can be erased in a few quick

rolls. Life becomes simple again.
If only poems were like

this. But even here, the choice
to entomb tiny spiders.

More often than not, I grant mercy—
I have buckets of time, poured

from the largest of drums
and more than a glimmer

of what small lives are like.
How easy it is to vanish

into the cream an entire body!
The whole house is falling

silent. Lashing the corners
of the world, cream on cream,

swiping on and off in thick stripes,
I am erased. The sun moves—

the brush paints its way into light.

Chris Lynch

Tom Boy Poet

Each Saturday you searched for sport
and sustenance after checking your tackle box
to find the right treble hook,
your favorite, the one with a bent point,
a straight eye, a long shank with
a shallow throat topped
with a tasty bait hoping to snag
a fresh-water catch.

In your wood boat, I sat, pondering
the number of fish that would dash by laughing
at your miscalculations—
ineffective baits, weights and bobbers
producing little yield.
I knew you weren't sure how
to earn a fresh catch when you removed
the bait with your hand,

spinning it around in the water.
Surely, you must have known with such antics, no
salmon, trout or bass could be
found, but only colorful carp for
which I grew so tired of
seeing. I longed to
wear dresses and feel like a Tammy;
not Tom nor a Tim.

Nikki Carr

Running Away and Coming Back

Winter captured the earth
when you left, the lawn
surrendered itself to mud and I
caught a train to where my life
was a stranger. The train
hugged the coast and the moon
lay a path to nowhere on the ocean.

While I was away my life
prowled the back step like
a wild starving dog. People fed it
scraps: slowly it grew fatter
and then at last it slept.

On the day I came back
(you never did) lightning
bolted heaven to earth and rainbows
rushed out from the rain
to meet the sun: assuage
the bruised clouds.
My house waiting for me
like a forgotten garden
welcoming spring.

Mran-Maree Laing

The Woman on the Island

Seabreath. You imagine roaring
over the barking of the seadogs
the black-dressed woman hopping from rock to rock
nine children dropping from her womb
and two bled out... in the moorland
in sight of the lighthouse brushing
the granite under blown stars...

It meant every year another child
pushed against the spume
and drunken stuttering of the light
hurt over grass and strict weather
the splutter and stink of the sea-oil
lamps blackening the close room
licked by wind, licked

by wind. And all for the stories: black light
the work horse that wouldn't
that swam, every year, to the mainland
the giving up of hard men
bending to their to sober duty
the child-cry of the sea-wind
the night-piercing of the Sun.

John Stokes

Tokyo

In a certain country unstable as its geology
    nights are charred paper.
Whispers transform them to flakes of ash
    the wind lifts and whirls like fairy skirts.
Burglars and the merely clumsy
    walk through walls as easily as dreams.
People have skin the colour of sun through honey.
Men neat as parcels of fish prepared by wives
    with downcast eyes know that humility
and hands are the only weapons
needed when respect is its own blade.
Camellias infuse their days with ceremony
    yield longevity and good health.
Art is the scalene triangle sun moon earth
    or carved on the teeth of dead giants
in a flowery and expensive complexity
also seen in the general's treatise on war.
A fondness for animals pervades.
Poets compose short verses about frogs
    a child's pony appears at table
a stray cat is taken in and fattened.
Counterfeit money is gifted to ghosts.

These things come in waves.

Jan Napier

Now You Know it All Goes on Beyond You Don't You (a cento for/after Matt Hetherington)

once more emptiness
makes itself known as form
   ('the usual clouds')

i am drinking
the sky through
     the top of my head

trees wave like coral, assenting,
stealing freely from the air
      (just to block out the house)

yoga is not in the fridge

the helpy pills = exit only
      (from some worse overthrow)

trying to save breaths, pouring
green tea (or tahini & honey, or
electric-period Miles) into the pain

bounce a sigh off
the wrecked angles of our room,
the impassable bed (full of holes)

(i carry my nothing
     between parenthetical arms)

unpack head, wash TV, suck on rocks

arriving at the necessary darkness
to think ...

the skyways
still knowing when not to stop,
no matter how you fold the map

Stu Hatton

Parts of the Furniture

Feet up, the fold-out camping chair theorist
scanned the horizon of ISS on
isstracker.com real-time,
by the glow of the screen on a River Red gum.

Second by second the circle it slid
down the slope of the graph of the orbital path.
Pixel by pixel the theorist deduced
they'd have all of Australia on view in ten minutes.

Rising, the fold-out camping chair theorist
hot-footed it down by the frog-song of night
to the knees in the river and ankles in mud;
then to the armpits, knees in the mud.

Washed the horizon out of her eyes,
leaned into a back float, and stared down the sky.

Brad Frederiksen

2015

her whole village
inside my kitchen
nonna's recipes

grey Melbourne skies
all my doodles growing
into flowers

Marisa Fazio

paddy field
rice plants sprout
on the moon

mountain mist
cars and buses greeting
with their headlights

Billy Antonio

Poetry & Place

        stargazing ...
        the outback camp oven
        glows red

        Ron C. Moss

now that the hedge is gone,
the neighbor's roses
stand tall

under porch eaves,
listening to rain —
moth ears

Jerome Gagnon

        dreaming of childhood -
        the Horries now flow in the
        other direction

        suburban rain
        the Rainbow Serpent wiggling
        through the waterholes

        Judit Katalin Hollos

blackberry winter
in the cemetery
a fresh grave

Elliot Nicely

Inland

the same path
  up the same hillside
    lambs follow the ewes

sheep country –
  passing clouds
    graze the hilltop

a sheep's year
  winding onto the spool
    the nights lengthen

dingo call by dingo call
  the terrain
    takes shape

Poetry & Place

shifting mist
  a rocky outcrop
    of wallabies

strands of fleece
  waving from fence wire –
    the long road home

wool skeins
  the shades of winters past
    sorted anew

Lorin Ford

deforestation talk a black butterfly loops above our heads

      third anniversary –
      the hotel where we stayed
      now only sky

Sandra Simpson

juniper the tether end of larksong

the forest under stars taking blankets

Alan Summers

Japan: a Haiku Sequence

cooling breeze
the curve of Sagami Bay
mimics the moon

rain softly falling
Kiyomizu-dera
in the clouds

morning light
on the centuries old roof
Kyoto spring

Joyce Joslin Lorenson

I am a seasonal vampire
I feed on summer.
Now, winter leeches my bones;
my joints are as supple
as the Tin Man's.

Karen Andrews

> jellyfish at sea
> the hanging mosquito net
> doesn't touch the bed

> imitating birds
> the pegs on my clothes airer
> hanging out for smalls

Nicola Scholes

limestone ruins
seasoning the hillside
pepper trees

> old farm midden
> digging through broken history
> an empty bottle
> still carries a message
> from the hand that tossed it

SB Wright

The Heat

crimson sunrise
the first signs of life
from the billabong

*a Bearded Dragon
skitters over loose shale*

ancient flame trees
their seed pods rattle
in the heat

*lightning strike
startled crows
take to the sky*

smoke on the flood plain
old-man roo stomps a warning

*rolling thunder
distant hills shimmer
in the haze*

- a rengay between Ron C. Moss and Simon Hanson

Petasus' and Petal's Next
(for Hanna in Holland and Tai in Aitutaki)

Were the sky to sink Petasus would write HELP
with red ink, when cyclones proceed to howl
Petal will draw with charcoal, as oceans rise

even further few will hear the roar of people
perishing in low-lying countries. A tardiness
to install solar, wind and thermal power

will see floods forcing dwellers to leave,
will hear Petasus and Petal mention their
brief calling for a fall in carbon emissions.

When draughts increase, withering crops,
taunting disease, fires out of control race
to consume a country's soul, do not wait

to find a person's bind to a bowl of rice
or a slice of bread. Tenable tomorrows,
most scientists said, rely on pollution-arrest.

Joyce Parkes

Crossroads

Our grand farmhouse stands at the crossroads of town that is no more. Only stone buildings remain - us and the old hall. The family that built the house were immigrants seeking freedom from religious troubles and the whims of petty kings in Central Europe. They brought with them new notions of faith and built things to last.

Clearing the *Bridal Creeper* from the *Honeysuckle* hedge one year, we came across an old beer bottle placed "just so" at its base. It put me in mind of a placation, to spirits or old household gods because even new faith carries old baggage.

>   dancehall tunes
>   shadows drink at the lights edge

The mayor, a descendant, laughed and told us of the old bylaw that said alcohol couldn't be taken within 200 yards of the hall.

SB Wright

Nullarbor at Night

Driving west into the sun
sears our eyes
and for millions of years and thousands of k's
this flat brittle saltbush
Crows scatter from shredded road kill
as we race to the end of the continent
In this oceanic scrub
it's flat out hard to gauge distance
   What seems a far off dot
comes upon the windshield in a flash
as car or splattered insect

This road has parts marked as a landing strip
with everyone hell bent on take-off
Bracing as hot engines rush by
a vortex of wind sweeps us in its wake
until the light starts to drain off the edge of the horizon
With the head-lights as blinding as the pitch black
and before the drivers nod, rollover
or the kangaroos dive bomb us,
we turn off and tuck into the bush

   When the camp fire dies
this mallee bush should come alive
But we see nothing of wombats, camels
or with relief, brown snakes in our swags
There's only the ghosts of exhausted truckies
scavenging the silence like dingos

To lay down on this old sea bed
is to be nakedly alone, exposed as insignificant
You could sleepwalk in any direction and never be found
Road trains leave contrails of light

Falling stars flare out like stones under wheels
Asteroids over take
as the roadside debris of space junk
piles up like the bones of dead cars and animals

It's time to let go of the wheel
and coast this milky highway
Tomorrow, sun waves will flood this surface
and we'll crawl the rest of this tiny foot path
The rush to get through has slowed us down
Flattened-out, engulfed in immensity
there's nothing here but space and time

Faith de Savigné

A Different Dawn

flying far
      and high
           and east
                a very long night's darkness
            seems
      enduringly
endless

  then – at last
  on a distant horizon
  deep velvety black
  nudges one lonely little
  burnt amber streak which
  - with a single timid toe -
  hesitantly reaches out
  to test the stratosphere
  for a quick reality check

  while this huge silver bird
  drones on and on and on
  carries us through vast space
  populated only by stars
  and five hundred mere passers by
  deceptively warm, secure
  encapsulated 32,000 feet
  above planet Earth traversing
  an invisible trajectory

  now a stage curtain opens

  new ephemeral light
  emerges from the gloom
  then swims upward

softly transforming
into dawn preliminaries -
that pale, pale blue hue
slowly tentatively
creating beacons of brightness
to push away the night at last

Traudl Tan

Land of Corn

Quetzalcoatl, feathered serpent god
became an ant trawled the mountains
to retrieve a grain that he gave to the people

this was a gift from the morning star
the first cob was a tiny vial of fruit
not like today's giant ears

corn was planted with beans and squash
and for protection from demons
orange and yellow flowers –

species later confirmed by science to hold
pesticidal properties

the crop
tilled by hand and hoe
harvested with a firm turn of the wrist

the grain
ground on stone by two strong arms
or carried to the mill each morning

the dough
shaped by folding clapping hands
placed on the griddle and turned

one tortilla at a time
hot to the fingers

colonial land grabs mining sugar cane
forced many cornfields to steep hillsides
laws called land reform
never served the small farmer

free trade only made things worse
corn imported from the northern neighbour
is of inferior quality
but the market rules

the many coloured cobs of Mexico
are further threatened by
a powerful seed monopoly
and genetically modified pollinators

children of the corn civilization
are now eating tortillas
manufactured from packaged flour

and women who grew up
in local corn economies
follow their menfolk across the border

to work perhaps in toxic
cash crop productions – tomato tobacco
or in sweat shops

they take their gods and goddesses with them
but even gods need a certain warmth to prosper
just as a future needs a past

today the museum is the temple
Chicomecóatl Seven Serpent corn goddess
sits back on her heels hands on her knees

she might have just straightened
from grinding the sacred maize

cobs of corn hang down her back
golden beads against the dark plaits
in basalt

Jacqueline Buswell

Inside Edward Hopper

Room in New York

We are in the front room upstairs. Just your usual rented brownstone. Apart from the piano. We only came to look at art and now we're inside a painting, held by the dark frame of the window at night. He's not talking to me. He's posing, pretending to read, stretching the paper into black and white shapes. I tinkle a few notes. Waiting. Electric light can be so brittle. It sharpens the space between us. My red dress has become the focal point in the picture, flesh tones soft against mahogany. Some guy is watching from the apartment across the street. He thinks I haven't noticed. I should pull the drapes, block out his angle of vision. But then we'd never get out.

Nighthawk

There's no stopping him: he went off in the middle of the night. Said he was going out for cigarettes. I'm not in this picture. There's no door, so I don't know if I could get in. Or how he will get out! He's sitting in there smoking, watching the couple at the counter, well the redhead anyway. The waiter is making small talk. Passing time. They are all shaped in a diner window. Separate, like extras in a movie. Artificial light freezes the frame, draining the colour. He's always looking for the story beyond the painted surface. But this time he's gone too far.

Brenda Saunders

Gone

On a real-estate site, I find photos
of the house where we lived, front door,
red step I bumped the pram over, day after
day. Down the hallway, hollow as a tunnel,
kitchen, bathroom, stark white, chrome,
no kids paintings on the fridge, no ducks
or colourful cups around the bath; yet

leaves of the Silver Birch still quiver
at windows. Into the sitting room, oak
boards stretch across an empty floor. Gone
is the carpet where children played. Gone
are the toy cars, toast crumbs, Lego…

like lifting a stone in the garden,
that space after woodlice have scattered.

Carolyn Abbs

2015

Heat, Flies and Cane Toads

Summer at Christmas was
heat, flies and cane toads.
We cousins raced
down the rickety wooden steps
edged with frogs
like a moss-robed choir
an overture for a tempest.
We hunted cane toads,
our mothers yelled but we
put them in ice cream containers
then set them free again.
They said we'd get warts
and eventually I did.

Some days we could smell the heat and
we played cricket
on the blistering grass
while the adults drank beer
and wine in the shade,
hurling belly laughs
that split our ears.

We drank coke and ate lollies and chips
and Grandpa's fresh-caught barra
that Grandma crumbed,
everything smelled like
claret and sunshine.
The undercurrents went over my head.

Sometimes after the cattle had been dipped
we had to pick ticks
out of the chenille bedspreads
as the mass crawling exodus

invaded the house.

The storms rolled in
thunder rumbled
and the lightning—
shards of electricity, flung by angry skies
to make the sugarcane shiver
while we inhaled ozone
and shrieked with glee.

And then it rained:
tapdancers on the corrugated roof.
The hypnotic drumming
drowned the chorus of frogs
singing on the stairs,
the cane toads
trysting in the thirsty grass.
Safely tucked in our de-ticked beds,
we dreamed of endless days
and tried to pretend
we would never grow up.

S. G. Larner

ICU

Everything here is on wheels.
Ready to move on a moment's notice.
Where to next?
Theatre?
Ward?
I know not home.
I lie here alone on cold, white sheets,
tethered to this world by tubes and machines.
They breathe for me and I cannot speak to thank them.
Mourners crying by the next bed.
Called late in the night to say their goodbyes.
For me it's checks around the clock.
Pathologists take blood soon.
Then rounds, all coats and serious optimism
Visitors next.
I squeeze their hands.
Trying to reassure.
Though, I know
I belong in this place.
The elite.
The sickest of the sick.
It has become my whole world.
My picture of home seems like a memory from a story.
Have I remembered it correctly?
Will the same person return?

Diana Jamieson

Distance Travelled Over Time Taken

for the brother I once had

      the shortest distance between two points
         is a straight line like linear time

            *

emotions attack me in a flurry of memories
& I, meant to be the 'strong' one,
am left drowning, trying to save you (me)
trying to reach back to you, to slow the moments
but all the time time moves forward

    now, that time has gone
      back there where we played our games
running down the street using our fingers as guns
making 'peyew' noises to fire a bullet
feeling the kickback, dodging the ricochet
           now the safety is off, you have grown
into something else &
I have to keep you, the dark creature, in my cross hairs

now if I think about the you back then I laugh & cry
        we were so innocent because
we believed we were so innocent

but no, we never had the milk-like innocence
that every child is owed, that is bestowed at their birth
      no, that spectre of our genetics was always looming
& we should have known we would have to pay
our mother's past due accounts

           *

there's a crash coming
        lightning has struck the horizon
& we're counting the seconds
to figure how far away it is

        & when the thunder comes
we'll wince & brace
for the aftershock

these are our lives now

Mark William Jackson

Crossing the Harbour Bridge

It's late and there have been some
shared intimacies this evening,
but now there is silence between us
as we drive along the road
that leads us home.

We approach the bridge,
allow it to hold us suspended
over the midnight water of the city
and it's easy not to feel
the weight of it all,
beams, hangers, pylons.
It's easy to ignore
the cantilevered arches
rising above us in cold steel,
two halves brought together
with rivets once white hot.

The bridge's purpose is clear.
It makes its own patterns,
oblique, repetitive, strangely beautiful,
the black sky peering from its ribs.

Above the arc
beams of light illuminate
a flock of silver gulls.
Ghostlike they swoop, free-wheel
snatch moths out of the night.

Vanessa Proctor

2015

A Passport

My parents were peculiar people,
at the time I thought them cruel:
not allowing television in our house.
When I complained, they liked to quote Groucho Marx
who had said that he found television very educational,
the minute someone turned it on,
he went into the library and read a good book.

Their house was furbished with shelves of books
murmuring *choose me, my friend*, to a lonely child.
I now realise with each book that they took down
and reverentially placed in my hands,
came a passport to places I will never visit
and things I will never see or do.

And yet it was me
who swam on my back across a lake in Wisconsin
with my pet racoon resting on my stomach;
who cycled along dirt roads with my masked friend leaning
forward from the basket,
his tiny hands gripping the handle bars,
his tail streaming back in the wind.

It was me who flew to the moon between the amber wings
of a giant moth,
landing in a valley of sand in light that changed unceasingly
from rose pink to green then violet.
Breathing was difficult; luckily I had my moon bell handy,
the perfumed orange flower that the moth had brought with
us to sustain me, weightless, as I bounded across the craters.

It was me, the rebellious, disobedient girl,
sent by my despairing father in Budapest
to my country cousins on the Hungarian plains to be tamed
but instead I climbed up into the rafters, swinging my long legs
in the air as I ate the sausages stored for winter.

It was me, the boy chimney sweep in the North Country,
climbing the dark flues, bearing the soot, my master's beatings
and prison as an old donkey withstands a hail storm.

It was me, one of the chattering elf children in a Russian forest
who commanded the magic tablecloth
to cover itself with the best dinner in the world
and then later, to turn itself inside out again,
resting clean and white on the table so that no elf had to do the
dishes.

My backyard held not spindly gumtrees but a gigantic tree
with pixies and fairies living in houses carved into its trunk,
a slippery-slide in the middle
and rotating lands at the top:
the Land of Birthdays, the Land of Do-As-You-Please.

Through time and space, I was never alone.
They are all there, these places I have been,
the places we will go, one day.
They are all there, waiting for me
to hand a book down from the bookcase
and quote Groucho.

S.E. Street

she was a nation. the loose-hipped, wet-lipped kind. opening her coal-seams, soaking down the blood of those slain, insane. keeping tight on treason and treachery. she bloomed through her dark history. driving to fyshwick, i used to see her, walking the blue-metal soft shoulder. winters she wore a kid-velvet top-hat. her clothes were complete layers shredded into invisible rags. her walk only a reluctant habit. her name was a word; spoken made you dirty, made you want to salt the slugs, boil the bulbs, core the turf. punish the dream, piss on the roses.

Monica Carroll

That I Might Love Differently

A gull shrieks. Wind-driven, discarded paper dips
and dances across the sand, touching now, there—
giddy with air's lift. I have wheeled you here

to sense the day. Wind blows hair into my face.
I press my ice cream to your lips. Against its melting
chill, you close your mouth. I adjust your hat and soften

to you. No jet ski sunders the afternoon. A wind
loses itself in play and you are too much for me.

***

The last morning, I leave you breathing. It is steady
labour. At a petrol station I stop to buy a juice, to drive
awake. Emerging from the Burnley tunnel, I taste

exhaust in the morning air, circle left to pass
beside the pillars of the Bolte bridge. Oxygen is
pressing your chest in and out. A monitor pegged

to your finger spells your life in code. At the exit
to Moreland Road loss hovers on both sides of your death.

Anne Elvey

On Neruda's Hill

    Bussed here
        they arrive they hope at the same

    unexpurgated sea
        view

    & sweet-smelling house of the rind
        reamed lemon and glycerin

    waves
        wafting to the Carmelites

    where pigeons after unanimous consent
        like swans made of felt

    remain dour
        and dogs for it just so happens

    they are sick of being dogs
        flop a sapped voltage

    on fresh tarmac
        and heat dawdles

    a craving turned acquiescence
        and I think

    how surely marvelous it would be
        to terrify a tourist with a fuchsia

    But tall grass has sprouted
        in the spot the stables stood

and green ink mildews the drain trench
    near where you wrote

Neftalí
    the day going from flute to flute

Jeff Schiff

Other People's Houses

Other people's houses are beautiful!
They are cream outside. Inside they are orange.
Somebody is playing guitar, and everyone
is wise and comfortable.

In other people's houses people hold parties.
There are jokes we haven't guessed.
The fears are more important.
There is more touch.
People care for themselves
just enough.

In other people's houses there live other people
dressing, undressing, speaking their thoughts
staring into eyes
asking
do you understand?

Other people's houses are shelter,
softening what we can't bear
with cream walls.
Our souls pass through.

Frances Olive

Stoplight Outside Hamburger Harry's, 2:00 a.m.

See the dark traffic of morning
disperse, the windshield blurred by rain
and the rhythmic tick of a turn signal.
See the bartender wipe down his bar
as if he were circling the moon's orbit.
The neon open sign in the window reflecting
blue and red against the pallor of his face.
See the television flicker a movie's end
and the waitress nod her goodbye –
no words between them now.
After years of repetition, this is the silence
they have come to. From Monday night's
football crowd to the middle-aged couple
who treat themselves every Thursday.
Reduced to the stripped down
directives of *two Coronas* and *order up* –
What more would they say?
Their thoughts come on
like the hot slap of meat on metal
and just as quickly fade. No words now.
Only the slow exhale of another night's routine,
the pull of a chain to quiet lights, the rattle of keys
to bolt out the sun.

Tina Schumann

2015

The Woodland Chapel

Maybe death smells like pine needles and tar
to the living, maybe only roofs pray
and eventually everything falls
you go out in a long boat, burning

being alive is a representation of living
you can taste everything in your last meal
nothing is next, you can't see it
maybe you remember it like clouds,

but all these vapours will be unmade,
like the universe, this one or any other one

the utilitarian rows are no more eternal
or more useful than porticos, or burnt viscera
names, dates, and signs

so the golden angel dances at the chapel entrance
like any plastic angel, the wood-worn columns
rot near the stone paving

if you could cross the water forever you would
but the water is rising here
and dying there, it all goes in a wave
a breeze in time, a time like now

you go out in a long moment, burning

Skogskyrkogården

Jill Jones

Retreat

I've been here before
   by the mint bush
     and the dry terracotta pots

with the weather-worn table
   a canvas for shadows
and the nails slowly sinking

   into the decking boards
til you can't see them at all
   in their tiny grave holes

The first time I wrote 'joy
   to wake in hut on hill'
but trip two and three

   are sadder
The sun is just as strong
the food is just as good

   and poetry still heals
but my eye alights
   on different things

On the dog bowl empty metal
   that used to be a saucepan
On leaf litter utterly meaningless

twigs and dirt and old grey leaves
    in need only of sweeping up
The way they catch in cracks

    and around the foot of pots
    is nothing but annoying
The broom's square head

    no use at all
and so they stay in little mounds
    a second ring of shadow

There is something sadder still
about the inside of a garden pot
    not meant to be seen

The glaze only token-rings the top
    and unevenly at that
The naked terracotta below

    bears its clay cellulite
and texta price tags
    crossed out black

Winter leaves its wake in pots
yellowed things die in them
    unremembered

waiting to be pulled up
    all-limbed in Spring
still clutching their death mound

to make way for a bright new Petunia
Why am I not looking at the view?
I've asked myself this

>   for two days in a row
> It is there as it was before
>   and somewhere I can hear
>
> the wattle beat its yellow drum

Sarah Rice

I'm More of an Amphetamines Girl, Myself

I. Seattle
When the first legal green shop opens
someone's granny lines up all night
to be the first inside.
Says it's every retiree's dream:
'Sleeping late and
smoking a bowl.'
This made the front page.

II. Humboldt County
At the festival
everyone showers nude.
I see one lady with
hairy armpits and shaved labia
and someone else says
'All r edibles are rooined
from water damage.
It's actually the worrrstuh.'

III. East Bay
His friend was murdered at 16
in a drive-by shooting
for mouthing off the drug gangs
on Facebook.
Now he keeps a gun
at home:
calls it self-defence.

IV. Los Angeles
All across the city
skinny bitches drunk on
champagne splits confess to

munching pills that
make them shit
instead of digest.

V. Calexico
Middle-aged internationals
cross down to Mexicali
to seek back-alley vets
selling something they call
'a choice
in the face of illness';
hoping on the way home
they'll pass as tourists.

Emma Rose Smith

Another Take on Recycling

The suburb of Newtown, Sydney,
developed rapidly after Camperdown Cemetery,
an Anglican graveyard, was established in 1848.
The publican of the Courthouse Hotel,
unhappy with the cemetery's proximity,
complained that during heavy rain
maggots were washed out through
fence palings on Lennox Street
and those not devoured by his duck
ended up in the pub's water supply.
Protein enhanced,
this gave a distinctive flavour
to water and beer
thereby presenting a positive case
for recycling
          even way back then.

Colleen Z Burke

Leaving the Monaro

For me there could be no final leaving
the greenish light, full and luminous
always a reminder of the underlying dark.

This is the country I go on dreaming in,
the bald hills, humped brown mountains,
a belt of grass and trees on either side

all part of a broken landscape
where parrots flew out from our ears,
the bleak cry of currawongs fracturing

the existence of sky.
The pull of our pared-back childhood,
linoleum and weatherboard house

equidistant from two schools
and a graveyard, snow falling on the woodheap
in winter. We were always cold

stuffing the crevices of our icy sheets at night
with spare clothing. The wind blew through
black stockings and uniforms, the slowly

emergent heat of classroom stoves no proof
against winter's bone. Weekends waiting
in the car, for our recalcitrant father

outside the Cooma Hotel, or weathering
"the regions", Guthega Dam and Adaminaby,
drowned Jindabyne, the hydro power stations

at Tumut, the recovering migrant workers,
toes blown off in the tunnels.
After the ice melted, hiking up the hill in summer

to the bleached sky and fall of blond valleys
the grasses and wattle, the snake-country,
escarpments and sandy river-stones,

I left, discovering the hard-edged city.
One last train-journey, past the track that signalled
the old SMA buildings, one flight by plane

was all it took. Sometimes in sleep I go back
to the feral, freezing high country
the colour of first light.

Margaret Bradstock

Only Decent Coffee in New York

Long hauled to a midtown Air BnB
to hear Patti Smith at the Met
reading Alice in Wonderland

and sore throat poetry,
because the night belonged to me
though I took 35 years to own it

Uptown, midtown & downtown
only Little Collins nailed me a latte
& a long black with crème for my dear friend

as Manhattan locked down, gridlocked
with The President in town
& the world's foreign ministers swarming the UN

Julie Bishop, head still wet with electoral victory
air kissed the American dream
pressed The President's hand

as the streets, the sky bristled black with NYPD
like a Batman movie, only real
so no Chaser's War could touch her.

Propped at Little Collins in a Lexington Ave groove
awake in my teenage dream

of walking the streets with Patti and Lou
Tony was my man, barista with the works

He wore no big straw hat, no PR shoes

2015

but I'd happily have slipped 26 dollars into his hand

for the sweet taste
of the only decent coffee
in New York.

Christine Burrows

Deep Cold Pockets

My mother was always cold
when entering Ripley Lake,
where vigilante eagles held watch from pines.
She wore a black wool bathing suit,
preserved by moth balls,
with a curved neckline of garter snake green.
She did not just jump in, as my Dad did,
or we, as children.
But inched painfully along, in tiny increments,
a crusader, her arms crossed across her chest.
Sometimes putting a baptismal thimbleful of
water over the blue fish flesh of her body.
That was when I learned some
things are too painful to watch.

Marilynne Thomas Walton

2015

This City

        This city hides its homeless.
         It destroys bus shelters
            where people have made
            home,
        to show the world
           we are a perfect city,
              a perfect place.

Long benches at railway stations,
         in the CBD, and in Hyde Park,
            are removed
        and replaced
with safe looking seats that
        do not allow for reclining
           horizontally.
    No sleeping allowed.
    We are a perfect city.

Beneath its veneer of beauty,
                    perfection,
     and ever developing
                construction
  for real estate
              satisfaction,
it is no perfect city.

Every city has an underbelly.
 The darkness of this place
   contrasts its beauty
and light.
     On and around the harbour
      everything seems happy,
       fun, and beautiful.

I am uplifted when I am there.

We have been moved on
    many times
from where we lived,
    in the
    inner city.

        Gentrification and real estate
           values dominated.

        The area was
    sterilised of any 'bohemian'
          life influence.
The streets are sterile
        of 'those' inner city types
    and now belong,
        predominantly at least,
           to those who
    saw it,
        wanted it,
and then destroyed it.

    Sterilised of controversial influence,
Political, social awareness, activists,
        artists, musicians, actors,
living on the edge,
        No more cafes with noticeboards
           lining their walls.
Buskers,
        none.
    Gone.
        Pushed out.
signs now say 'No busking without permission'
    in the CBD railway tunnels.
        I busked there,
           years ago.
                The acoustics are nice.

2015

There is not music there now.
Only the sound of footsteps,
approaching and leaving.

Hospitals are closed, and changed into
ritzy apartment blocks.
I can count five without any difficulty.

At one time,
in the year before the madness of the
real
estate wave began,
I lived behind the Opera Centre,
an arts rehearsal space in the inner city.
My two house mates and I
enjoyed the sound of the
singers' practice,
and
delighted
in the arias drifting
into our small garden backing onto the centre.
Sandwiched comfortably between this arts space and
Belvoir St Theatre
just a few doors up on the other side of our street,
it was a cultural atmosphere,
and sometimes a play spilled out
onto the street
at night
between our place and theatre door.
...The artistic inner city...
I found my city niche here.
But all too soon,
it was lost to the real world.
The real
estate
world.

Where I live now,
>   artists, musicians, political activists,
>   all are in the surrounding area.
>   a green belt of consciousness,
>   radicalism and sub-culture,
>   living side by side with conservative
>   establishment precedents.
Where I live,
>   is not a bad place
>   all in all.
Multicultural diversity, a world melting pot.
>   I am connected, to some extent.
>   At times.
There is some element of community
>   that I feel a part of.

>   Even if I just hang out for a while
>   in a cafe, I can see it
>   is there,
>   and I feel a part of it all.

>   But real estate values are dominating again.
>   And the survival of the fittest and strongest
>   is the battle cry,
>   in a battle
>   I cannot compete.
...We live in an inner suburb,
>   for nearly four years now.
>   We are now the only renters
>   in a row of seven, semi-detached houses,
>   worth more than
>   they could possibly be worth.

>   The sense of the place has changed,
>   even in these few years.
>   Gentrification is on its way.

It has almost arrived.
It is already partially here.
And we will be gone soon enough.

Julie Storer

Blue

Sometimes you think you're safe, you know? Like no one can touch you, put their stuff on you, take you down real low. Like the other day, I was standing in the sunshine, looking good in my hottie pants, having fun with the other girls. I was thinking, I have almost enough to leave now, go where the sun makes you feel clean, like blue water, where you can wake up clean between clean sheets, the blue clean of Clorox and island getaways and movie-star eyes. I could maybe be a hostess at one of those Hollywood restaurants, the ones where the chefs serve little bits of things in weird shapes and people tip you just because you smile right. Thank you very much, I'd say, and be gracious and charming, and my boss would smile and say, You're the best we've ever had, Angie. And the restaurant would have pale blue chairs and drapes, sweet as baby clothes, and I'd sing softly after closing, just to myself, because I'd be so happy. I'd be so happy, I'd sing all the way home. I'd sing and sing because I was so lucky. Lucky, lucky me.

Janis Butler Holm

2015

42 Memories

1977 brings marriage
and moving.
Fifties fibro
at $30 000.
Hand me down
furniture
and scrubbing.
1980s renos
two bedrooms
made over for girls.
Mortgage ended
driveways cobbled.
Gardens of
camellia
and azalea.
Barbecues
and family.
Guinea pigs
and pet ducks.
Additions
and paint,
Cladding
then porches.
Landscaping,
millennium
workplace-
Students swing
on gates.
Kitchen
and bathroom.
Empty nest
re-arranging.
cacti beds

and pots.
Re-paints.
Re-decorating.
Re-discovery.
Retirement
awaits
more memories.

Alison Miller

The Flooded Field

Past the lotus-choked pond,
past boulders, anxiety, signs
telling you to turn back
past sarsaparilla and mayapple,
you find a path

At the first gate, leave names behind
and find rustling
above the emptying mind

At the next gate, leave behind
clock-time and memory
Follow the paths of animals

At the third gate
a great gale of open space
a curl of wind
        that ripples the flat mirror
of the flooded field

Ankle-tipping on its edge you pause
to watch the gold and black wings
of a butterfly who takes flight
              as the Riverside Line
rumbles beyond the silent water

Frances Donovan

Christmas Email

The way I used to go down to the mailbox –
sometimes two or three times –
pick out the snails,
make a quiet white nest for a letter.

Wes Lee

Do You Remember...

There was that time
In western Wyoming
Or was it Montana
The truck was broke
Down in some nameless town
You had the cab jacked up
To get to the monster of an engine
We made up beds under
The stars beside the trailer
Mom fretted back and forth
Between you elbow deep in the diesel
And us, your babes, asleep
Or pretending sleep under
A blanket of clear night sky
And stars so vividly bright
I still swear I saw the rings
Of Saturn that night

Was it that same trip
Or another, there were so many
They ran together
We stopped along a lonely
Length of highway
Somewhere to somewhere
With a whole lot of nowhere
In between
Everything was dusty brown
Not the wet green of home
Off the side of a forgotten path
A marker was placed
To tell of the cowboys who rode
That way pushing cattle to market
Once upon a time

We drove the trail with you
Behind the wheel of your big rig
Trying to imagine those
Who had only their horses
And nerves
You, behind the wheel, were equal to them

Nina Longfield

Ghost Town
(Fremantle)

This town is a realm for ghosts.
Its streets are dusty,
grimed with summer dirt,
slick with a patina of despair.
Coffee shops proliferate
yet Papa's squats like a rotten tooth
empty of its last incarnation.
The town is soiled.
Even the 'Doctor' cannot breathe
fresh life into the dark corners.
Ghosts of more bustling times
linger and drift from bare shop fronts,
across hot pitted pavements,
into the doorways of pubs and
past blank windows that mirror
day trippers with their vacant eyes.

Veronica Lake

Her Country

Fidgety fingers peel scabs
of wood. Varnish blisters, flakes
off the desks, festers. We whisper
as lids drop shut. The teacher inflicts
the stick against the board; *a e i o u*
we enunciate and release sweaty legs
from the seat.

A boy jabs a compass into his ruler and spins
it like a helicopter blade to suspend
boredom. He holds his hand
steady and braces for the brunt
of its back, its side ink-black,
as the termagant administers
metric discipline. She whips
her wounds, unholy woman
in white, and dishonours
her flapping bat-winged habit.

Blurted out as beliefs she brandishes
prejudice: pick pick pick. Sticks and stones
and words hurt. *Dirty disgusting do-it-
again;* my dark-eyed classmate doesn't see
it coming. The stain of judgement day veils
ankle socks, pigtails and play. We cringe
over counting rods in the middle of maths.

Bright shiny girl, bones
of her country, millennia before
our society insinuates children
into the system and difference
disappears offshore.

Colleen is her name, remember
lank limbs as she sits. Her head
hangs; I wait, until it lifts and shift
my eyes to hers.

Gabrielle Rowe

Sell and Regret, But Sell

An old cocky's advice: "Kim, a farm's like two dice,
you can roll and lose twice, that's all.
On a farm with a debt, you must never forget:
you should sell and regret - but sell.
When the wool price drops down and a permanent frown
creases cheeks like a town-scuffed shawl,
when the rain's overdue, then your choices are few:
feed the sheep till it's through - or sell.

"You can lighten off first before prices are worst;
to buy grain is to thirst for pain.
If the money's so tight that your sleep's wrecked all night,
though it hurts, you'll be right - to sell.
When the barley won't grow, stony rivers won't flow
and dry knees crackle low for rain;
before fuel bills fall due, city brothers blame you
and the grasses turn blue - please sell.

"As resilience bleeds, your accounts run to weeds.
Hear your child when he pleads, or wilt.
There's a life past the gate but don't leave it too late -
stand tall and stand straight - and sell.
My girl, drought's not a test, folk and paddocks need rest;
count your blessings is best, no guilt.
It's the end of my game; I've no blame and no shame.
When the trigger points came - I sold."

Robyn Sykes

Mother Roux

Five deep,
her skirts laden
with the sweat
of three hundred
days, hands
glove bound with
slick of salt,
blood of life,
water how the
soap pooled in
the bottom of
the tub, chain
rusting to the
enamel with
the grace of
thieves, her
face cracked
six times with
the lines of
fish and shrimp
that flow through
her fingers,
death by death,
her spirit boot
clad as her
eyes look out
to sea for one
last breath of
how pink cries.

Katarina Boudreaux

On His Wedding Day

We were wondering if you could write something
but the noise of it is too much to find a word in

the squeal of the microphone on the wind-slapped beach
the panic of the grandmother finding her seat

the sea between the two of you won't stop crashing

Vows somewhere up with the helium
the ring knuckling

words aren't steady enough
to tell these things

Look out at the ocean wearing holes
in the sides of the country

how plants have clamped down around it
how the sky stares but doesn't reach it

Alice Allan

Grant's Picnic Ground, Sherbrooke Forest

Corellas hang in bare branched trees
like unexploded hand grenades. Their heads
are filled with dangerous ideas.

Outraged squawks force others
from the feeding ground,
conquered long ago.

Visitors cook lamb on little
barbecues, drink beer and wine, eat sandwiches
and cakes, feed
the raucous mob.

Turn to the surrounding forest -
mountain ash, sixty metres high,
wattles, creeks, muddy paths

where rosellas nest, lyre birds dissemble, magpies
delight in their own voices, wrens
shyly vanish, bowers abound -

forget the crowd of corellas
whose anxious eyes igore the seeds
on nearby trees, their voices uplifted,

More! More!

Penny Gibson

The Smile of the Orange-Robed Monk

The smile of the immigration official as he directs you to the queue to purchase your entry visa. How you pass a guardian lion carved from stone, proudly displayed in the Arrivals Hall.

The smile of the guesthouse owner as he hands you the slip of paper with internet password and offers you a mangosteen to have with your breakfast.

The smile of the teenage girl selling photocopied versions of *Cambodia Year Zero* and *First they killed my father* outside the ruins of Thommanon. The way she speaks with an almost perfect American accent. How she sells you a copy of the *Lonely Planet* guide to Cambodia, minus the fold-out maps.

The smile of the seven-year-old who convinces you to buy an origami grasshopper made from folded palm fronds. The different kind of smiles from her brothers and sisters, who cajole you into buying postcards and key-rings.

The smiles of the *pinpeat* players seated on a mat on the path to Ta Phrom. How they beat *sampho* and *skor thon* and lift the mood of the tourists walking towards the temple. How as you approach you notice one of the musicians is blind and each of them carries a stump for an arm or leg.

The smile of the bus driver navigating the road to Phnom Penh. How he calls out in Khmer before screening karaoke on the small TV. How as he passes a field fringed with palms he looks back and calls out in English that the place was once a killing field.

The smile of the young tuk-tuk driver as he spots you through the throng at the Central Market. The way he beats older tuk-

tuk drivers in getting to you. How he barks at an older driver who tries to outbid his offer. The way the young driver leans on his tuk-tuk outside your hotel in the morning. How he smiles as he asks if you want sightseeing.

The smile of the orange-robed monk as he points you in the direction of the stupa containing an eyebrow hair of the Buddha. The way you climb the staircase leading to the low-ceilinged shrine of rough-hewn rock. How inside you find a figure of the Buddha, behind it a mandala of radiating neon lights.

Frank Russo

Acknowledgements

Firstly, we'd like to thank all the writers from across the world who supported the anthology with their poetry. The variety and care shown with both theme and form has kept the project exciting every step of the way.

Taking a huge project like an anthology from start to finish represents hours upon hours of hard work, not just from the two of us as editors and publishers, but also from the writers who toiled before we even saw the poems. We're proud of the 2015 Poetry & Place Anthology and appreciate the trust poets have given us when it comes to publishing their work. (In regards to regionalisms (spelling for example) we have attempted to preserve these as per the individual author's national language conventions.)

We want to thank our team of readers, proofers and especially Louis at Indigo Forest Designs for creating such a fantastic cover. We'd also like to thank who spread the word about this anthology via social media or word of mouth, especially during calls for submissions.

To writers, please keep an eye out for future calls for submissions. To readers, thanks for buying, sharing or simply reading this - we hope that you enjoy the poems within!

Ashley & Brooke
Editors

Contributor Biographies

A. S. Patric is the author of *Black Rock White City*, *Bruno Kramzer*, *Las Vegas for Vegans*, *The Rattler & other stories*, and a collection of poetry: *Music For Broken Instruments*.

Alan Summers, a *Japan Times* award-winning writer, appears in various leading haiku anthologies, and recently on *NHK World* (Japanese television). He adores French, Italian, Japanese, and Indian food although not necessarily at the same time. Website: www.withwords.org.uk

Alice Allan's poetry has appeared in *Cordite*, *Rabbit*, *Southerly* and *Australian Book Review*. You can find more of her writing at aliceallan.net.

Alison Miller is an emerging writer and proud suburban Revesby resident who has raised two, now-adults with autism, whilst writing short stories and poetry about life, love, death and domesticity. My love of words, semantics and literature has made my unpredictable life both successful and satisfying.

Amelia Walker has published three poetry collections and three books on teaching poetry in the primary school context. She recently completed her PhD through the University of South Australia, where she currently works as a casual lecturer and tutor.

Andrew Phillips from Brisbane is currently searching for poetry in the Sacramento River and Northern Californian mountains. He's a father of five and proud poet of one of the pieces in this fine collection.

Anne Elvey's recent publications include *Kin* (Five Islands Press, 2014), shortlisted for the Kenneth Slessor Poetry Prize, and *This Flesh That You Know* (Leaf Press, 2015). Managing editor of *Plumwood Mountain: An Australian Journal of Ecopoetry and Ecopoetics*, Anne holds honorary appointments at Monash University and University of Divinity.

Barbara A Meier recently moved to Gold Beach, OR from Medford, OR to teach full day kindergarten. Adventure HO! She has poems published in *Poetry Pacific*, *Miller's Pond Journal*, *Cactifur*, and *River Poet's Journal*.

Ben Walter is a Tasmanian writer of lyrical poetry and fiction. His work has appeared in *Island*, *Overland*, *Griffith Review*, *Southerly* and a range of other journals. He was recently shortlisted for Overland's 2014 Judith Wright Poetry Prize.

Benjamin Dodds is the author of *Regulator* (Puncher & Wattmann Poetry, 2014). His work has appeared in Best Australian Poems 2014, Antipodes: Poetic

Responses, Stars Like Sand: Australian Speculative Poetry and on Radio National's Poetica program. His current project is a verse novel exploring the boundaries of scientific research.

Billy Antonio is at present an elementary grades teacher. His short story, The Kite, has been broadcast on 4EB-FM, 98.1, Brisbane, Australia. Some of his fiction and poetry have been published in the fiction anthology *Only Men Please*, *World Haiku Association Haiga Contest*, *Mainichi Daily News*, *Rose Red Review*, *Tincture Journal*, *Red River Review*, *Penwood Review*, *Akitsu Quarterly*, *Three Line Poetry*, *Hedgerow: a journal of small poems*, *Poetry Quarterly*, *Asahi Shimbun*, *Sharpening the Green Pencil*, *New Mexico Wilderness Alliance Wild Guide 2011*, *Anak Sastra*, *Philippines Free Press*, *Philippine Graphic*, *Ani*, *Liwayway*, *Sirmata*, *Tinig* and *The Literary Apprentice*. He lives in Casantiagoan, Laoac, Pangasinan with his wife Rowena and his daughter Felicity.

Brad Frederiksen (born 1968) has been defined by a variety of technical and managerial roles in the vending industry for the best part of 30 years. He took himself to university in 2004 intending to qualify as a school teacher. His mentors identified him rather as a poet and philosopher.

Brenda Saunders is a Sydney poet and artist. She has written three collections of poetry, her latest *the sound of red* (Gininderra Press 2013) features prose poems inspired by art and travel. Her work has appeared in selected anthologies and was included in *Best Australian Poems 2013* (Black Ink). Brenda was a finalist in the Aesthetica Poetry Prize UK 2014.

Carolyn Abbs is a Western Australian poet published in journals and anthologies such as *Westerly*, *Cordite*, *Rabbit*, *Writ Poetry Review*, *Axon: Creative Explorations*, *The Best Australian Poems 2014*, and *ABR*. Her PhD is from Murdoch University where she taught in the School of Arts for a number of years.

Carolyn Gerrish is a Sydney poet. She has published five collections of poetry. The latest is 'The View From the Moon' (Island Press, 2011). She runs creative writing classes at the WEA and community organisations. She often performs her work. Currently she is working on her sixth collection.

Caitlin Thomson just moved for the 15th time. Her work has appeared in numerous places, including: *The Literary Review of Canada*, *Radar*, *Going Down Swinging*, and the anthology *Killer Verse*. Her second chapbook *Incident Reports* was recently released by Hyacinth Girl Press.

Chris Lynch is a writer and teacher based in Melbourne. His poetry has appeared in *Tincture Journal*, *Cordite*, *Apex Magazine*, *Blackmail Press*, *Islet*, *Peril Magazine*, and *Stars Like Sand: Australian speculative poetry*, among others. He is working on his first collection of poetry, and blogs occasionally at www.chrislynch.com.au.

Christine Burrows is a Melbournian kiwi who spent the early 80's in Sydney. Early poems appeared in NEOS, P76 and the Angry Women's Anthology. Since re-emerging in 2013 Christine's work has appeared in Melbourne Spoken Word's Zine & *Audacious Vol 1* and *Offset 15*. She frequents open mics in Melbourne. Her poetry spits and bites at political lunacy and social (in)justice and explores life's deeply personal challenges. Her first book *Delirium nostalgia* was published recently.

Colleen Z Burke, poet and author, has published eleven poetry books and her most recent collection is *Splicing air*. She is also co-editor of *The Turning Wave: Poems and Songs of Irish Australia*. *Doherty's Corner* is her biography of Australian poet Marie E.J. Pitt.

Diana Jamieson was born in Sydney and now lives and works in Brisbane with her husband Trent. She has been writing poetry for years and won a poetry competition while at school. When not writing poetry she works as a Primary School Teacher.

Duncan Richardson is a writer of fiction, poetry, haiku, radio drama and educational texts. He teaches English as a Second Language part time.

Elliot Nicely resides in the United States of America where he works as an English teacher. His poetry has appeared in more than a dozen anthologies across four continents. He is still pursuing all of the answers to all his questions, but he hopes not all of them will be answered.

Emma Rose Smith writes manic poetry, smelly-lady nonfiction, and fiction that overuses the word 'ululate'. She is cycling her way to firmer thighs, and sometimes drafting a novel. Her thesis is on the power dynamics of 'hysteria' in Aus-postcolonial women's writing.

Faith de Savigné Faith de Savigné lives in Kings Cross where we don't look back because we're not going that way. She has had her poetry published in Australia (*Best Australian Poetry, Earthly Matters*) as well as the USA.

Fiona McIlroy has taught in far East Gippsland while raising three children. Poetry has always been her passion, and she published two collections (Ginninderra Press) and won the HRAFF Poetry Prize 2009. She was published in *Poetry DÁMour* 2014 & 2015. Fiona runs the Poets Train Canberra to Sydney during Poetry Week.

Frances Donovan's work has appeared or is upcoming in such publications as *Marathon Literary Review, Dirty Chai, 823 on High, Ishka Bibble, Oddball Magazine, Incessant Pipe, Lyrical Somerville, PIF Magazine, The Writer, Chronogram,* and *Gender Focus*. She curated the Poetry@Prose reading series and has appeared as a featured reader at numerous venues in the Northeast. She once drove a bulldozer in a GLBT Pride parade. You can find her climbing hills in

Roslindale and online at www.gardenofwords.com.

Frances Olive writes poetry, short stories and something in between. Her work has appeared in literary journals in Australia and the US. She completed her doctoral studies in philosophy at the University of Sydney.

Frank Russo's collection poetry *In the Museum of Creation* was published by Five Islands Press in 2015. His recent writing has been published in the journals *Southerly, Contrappasso, Cactus Heart, pacificReview* and in anthologies in Australia and North America.

Gabrielle Rowe is a Postgraduate at the University of Sydney who loves compassion and humour. *Her Country* was shortlisted for the ACU 2015 Prize for Poetry and included in the chapbook: *Peace, Tolerance and Understanding*. Her poem 'Fast' was published in *HERMES 2015 – Issue 109*. Twitter: @GabrielleEspoir

Guy Traiber studies Sociology & Political Science and Chinese Medicine and finds that they all relate to poetry and to each other. His writing has appeared in (very) few journals and rejected by many. Speak to him about anything: 013m@yahoo.com

Irene Wilkie has published two books of poetry, *Love and Galactic Spiders* and *Extravagance*, both with Ginninderra Press. The latter won a Highly Commended Award in the ACT Writing and Publishing Awards 2014. Her work has been widely published in many anthologies and journals. She is a member of the Kitchen Table Poets, Shoalhaven and can be contacted through www.kitchentablepoets.com.au

Ivy Alvarez is the author of two poetry collections: *Disturbance* (Seren Books, 2013) and *Mortal* (2006). A recipient of writing residencies from MacDowell Colony, Hawthornden Castle and Fundación Valparaiso, her work appears in journals and anthologies in many countries, with individual poems translated into Russian, Spanish, Japanese and Korean. www.ivyalvarez.com

Professional editor **J. Todd Hawkins** writes and lives in Texas. His poetry has appeared or is forthcoming in *AGNI, American Literary Review, Louisville Review*, and elsewhere. He holds an MA in Technical Communication, loves Mississippi Delta blues, and routinely loses to his wife at Mortal Kombat while the kids sleep.

Jacqueline Buswell was born in rural NSW, and completed a Bachelor of Arts at the Australian National University. She lived in Mexico for more than 20 years. After returning to Australia, she has lived in Sydney. Jacqueline has worked as a journalist, teacher of English as a second language and Spanish-English translator and interpreter. She completed a Masters of Arts in Creative Writing at the University of Sydney in 2011. Ginninderra Press published her first book of poems, *Song of a Journeywoman*, in 2013.

James Croteau lives in Kalamazoo, Michigan with his partner of 30 years, Darryl. He grew up gay and Catholic in the U.S. south. His poems have appeared in *Assaracus, Haibun Today,* and *New Verse News* among others. His first chapbook will come out in 2016 from Redbird Chapbooks. talkingdogsholymen.blogspot.com.

Jan Napier lives near the Indian Ocean. Her work has been published in *Westerly, Famous Reporter, Best Love Poems 2013, The Stars Like Sand,* and *Poetry New Zealand,* as well as other journals and anthologies both in Australia and overseas. Her poem 'Turned On' won the Creatrix Prize For Poetry 2014.

Jane Downing's poetry has been published in journals including *Rabbit, Eureka Street, Social Alternatives, foam:e, Windmills, Poetrix, the Canberra Times,* and *Best Australian Poems* (2004).

Jane Williams is a poet and writer based in Tasmania.

Janis Butler Holm lives in Athens, Ohio, where she has served as Associate Editor for _Wide Angle_, the film journal. Her prose, poems, and performance pieces have appeared in small-press, national, and international magazines. Her plays have been produced in the U.S., Canada, and England.

Jeff Schiff is author of *Anywhere in this Country* (Mammoth Press), *The Homily of Infinitude* (Pennsylvania Review Press), *The Rats of Patzcuaro* (Poetry Link), *Resources for Writing About Literature* (HarperCollins), and *Burro Heart* (Mammoth Press). His work has appeared internationally in more than seventy periodicals, including *Grand Street, The Ohio Review, Poet & Critic, The Louisville Review, Tendril, Pembroke Magazine, Carolina Review, Chicago Review, Hawaii Review, Southern Humanities Review, River City, Indiana Review,* and *The Southwest Review*. He has taught at Columbia College Chicago since 1987.

jenni nixon is a Sydney poet and performer. Readings at many diverse venues includes Sydney Writers Festival with the Harbour City Poets. Recent poetry published with *Spineless Wonders, Southerly, Overland, Homeward Bound* (India). Her new book of poetry *swimming underground* (Ginninderra) was published in September 2015.

Jenny Blackford's poems have been published in *APJ, Westerly, The Pedestal Magazine* and more. Her poetry prizes during 2014 included first place in the Humorous Verse section of the Henry Lawson awards, second in the W.B. Yeats Poetry Prize for Australia and third in the ACU Prize for Literature. In late 2013, Pitt Street Poetry published her chapbook of cat poems, *The Duties of a Cat*.

Jerome Gagnon has lived for most of his life in the San Francisco Bay Area, working as a teacher, tutor, and journalist. A graduate of San Francisco State University's creative writing program, his poetry has appeared in the M*adison Review, archaeopteryx, Japanophile,* and *Haiku Presence,* among other journals, while articles and reviews have been published in newspapers and online.

Jill Jones' eighth book, *The Beautiful Anxiety* (Puncher and Wattmann 2014), won the 2015 Victorian Premier's Prize for Poetry. A new book, *Breaking the Days*, is due from Whitmore Press in late 2015. She is a member of the J.M. Coetzee Centre for Creative Practice, University of Adelaide.

Jill McKeowen Jill McKeowen has lived in many places, but currently calls Newcastle home. Her poems are in *Grieve* 2015 (Hunter Writers Centre) and *Indelible*, the 2015 Poetry at the Pub anthology. She teaches academic writing at the University of Newcastle.

John Stokes is an international poet and author. His work is published widely in Europe, the U.S.A., Japan and Australia and extensively anthologised. He has won or been shortlisted for many major prizes and represented Australia at international festivals. His latest book is *Fire in the Afternoon* (Halstead Press, 2014).

John Upton believes poetry can say more with less. John began as a journalist, made a switch to drama and wrote professionally for TV and stage for 27 years, after which he was able to retire and focus exclusively on poetry.

Jonathan Hadwen is a Brisbane writer who has been haunting the various halls of SpeedPoets open mic since 2008. His work has appeared in *Westerly*, *fourW*, *Mascara*, and *Stand Magazine* as well as other publications in Australia and overseas. He is currently the co-editor of the online poetry journal *foam:e*, and helps out with the Queensland Poetry Festival.

Joyce Joslin Lorenson lives in Rhode Island, U.S.A., grew up on a dairy farm and records the daily happenings in nature around her rural home. She has been published in several print and electronic journals.

Joyce Parkes is published in *Axon, Plumwood Mountain Journal, Regime, Cordite, foam:e, Abridged, Overland, Westerly, the Broadkill Review, Pen International, The Best Australian Poems* 2005 (UQP) and in similar publications dedicated to literature and the arts in the UK, Finland, Canada, Germany, the US, New Zealand, Northern Ireland and Greece.

Judit Katalin Hollos is a Hungarian teacher, writer, translator and freelance actress. She was educated at Budapest University, majoring in Swedish literature and language. Her articles, short stories, poems and translations have been featured in two languages in anthologies and literary magazines in Hungary and abroad.

Julie Storer is a musician and songwriter and also puts words into poetry. She has a B.A. in music and drama and recently attained her PhD. Her arts-based research thesis explored stories of learning though health, the body, place and creativity, focusing on merging the areas of creativity, health and education.

Karen Andrews is an award-winning writer of both short stories and poetry, author, editor and publisher. Her work has appeared in many publications throughout the country. Her blog (www.karenandrews.com.au) is a two-time finalist in the Best Australian Blogs competition and she regularly conducts workshops on the subject. She lives in Melbourne and can be found on Twitter (@KarenAndrewsAU).

Karen Murphy is studying a PhD in Digital Poetry at Curtin University. In 2012 and 2013 she coordinated the WA Poetry Festival and is an invited artist for the 2015 National Young Writers' Festival. She has published poems in literary journals and anthologies including *The Australian Poetry Journal* and *Writ Poetry Review*.

Katarina Boudreaux is a writer, musician, composer, tango dancer, and teacher - a shaper of word, sound, and mind. She recently returned to New Orleans after residing in Texas, Connecticut, and New York. She has been published in *The Bacon Review, PANK, SNReview, Blueline, New Jersey Underground,* and *Calliope*. New work is forthcoming in *Corvus, Far Away Places, The Sundial Review,* and *YAY!LA*.

Kevin Gillam is a West Australian writer with three books of poetry published. Most recently, he has been awarded winner of the Sawtooth ARI Writing Prize (Poetry), the 'Open Your Mind' Poetry Competition, and the 'Interstellar Poetry Prize' for Speculative Poetry.

Koraly Dimitriadis is a storyteller through various mediums such as poetry, writing, theatre, performance, acting and screen. She is a freelance columnist with work published in *The Age, Daily Life, Sydney Morning Herald, Rendezview* and *The Saturday Paper*. Koraly is the author of the acclaimed *Love and F**k Poems* with rights sold to the UK and Greece.

Les Wicks has toured widely and seen publication in over 300 different magazines, anthologies & newspapers across 22 countries in 11 languages. His 11th book of poetry is *Sea of Heartbeak (Unexpected Resilience)* (Puncher & Wattmann, 2013), his 12th (a Spanish selection) *El Asombrado* (Rochford St, 2015). http://leswicks.tripod.com/lw.htm

Lorin Ford is haiku editor and publisher of the on-line journal, *A Hundred Gourds*. Her haiku have featured in journals and anthologies worldwide since 2005, including the ground-breaking anthologies *Montage:The Book, Haiku 21, Haiku in English* and *Where the River Goes*. Her collection, *a wattle seedpod*, is the first by an Australian to win a first place in the Haiku Society of America Merit Book Awards.

Margaret Bradstock has six published collections of poetry, including *The Pomelo Tree* (winner of the Wesley Michel Wright Prize) and *Barnacle Rock* (winner of the Woollahra Festival Award, 2014). Editor of *Antipodes: poetic responses to 'settlement'* (2011), in 2014 Margaret won the national Earth Hour poetry competition and the Banjo Paterson Award.

Margaret Owen Ruckert, educator and poet, is mostly travelled through food. Her book *You Deserve Dessert* contained 110 sweet food poems, while *musefood* won an IP Poetry Book of the Year. A previous winner of NSW Women Writers National Award, Margaret gives writing workshops as Facilitator of Hurstville Discovery Writers.

Marilynne Thomas Walton, retired as a librarian in New York City and St. Paul, Minnesota, where she now lives. Her poetry has appeared in numerous anthologies and journals, recently in *NODIN POETRY ANTHOLOGY*, published in 2015. She enjoys writing in her little red house with the big green spruce tree.

Marisa Fazio writes poetry and short prose. Her writing has been published in numerous anthologies and journals in Australia and internationally. She lives in Melbourne.

Mark Miller's first book of poems, *Conversing with Stones*, won the Anne Elder Award in 1989 and his second, *This Winter Beach*, was published in 1999. A manuscript of his third book, *Scanning the Horizon*, was runner-up in the 2010 ACT Poetry Prize. Mark's poems have been published widely in newspapers and journals, and online, both in Australia and overseas. He lives on the south coast of New South Wales.

Mark William Jackson's work has appeared in various journals including; *Best Australian Poems, Popshot, Going Down Swinging, Cordite, Rabbit Poetry Journal, Verity La* and *Tincture*. For more information visit http://markwmjackson.com

Michele Seminara is a poet, editor and yoga teacher from Sydney. Her writing has appeared in many online and print publications, and her first poetry collection, *Engraft*, was recently published by Island Press (2016). Michele is also the managing editor of online creative arts journal *Verity La*.

Monica Carroll has been published in a variety of journals and anthologies such as *Picaro Press Poetry, DecomP, Poetrix, Cordite, Block, Antipodean, Idiom* and *New Australasian Writing*. She is a researcher at the University of Canberra. In addition to writing, Monica likes to mix concrete.

Mran-Maree Laing is an award winning Sydney poet, essayist and fiction writer. She has published poetry in a range of journals and publications including *Best Australian Poems 2015, Meanjin* and *Cordite*. She is currently enrolled in a Masters of Creative Arts at UTS, Sydney.

Nathanael O'Reilly is the author of *Distance* and the chapbooks *Suburban Exile* and *Symptoms of Homesickness*. Over one hundred of his poems have appeared in journals & anthologies, including *Antipodes, Australian Love Poems, Blackmail Press, Cordite, fourW, LiNQ, Mascara, Snorkel, Social Alternatives, Tincture, Verity La* and *Windmills*.

Nicola Scholes is the author of *Dear Rose* (2009), and was shortlisted for the 2013 Arts Queensland Thomas Shapcott Poetry Prize. Her most recent work appears in *foam:e* (Issue 11), *still heading out: An Anthology of Australian and New Zealand Haiku* (paper wasp, 2013), and *Under the Basho* (December 2014).

Nikki Carr lives and writes in California and her work has appeared in various publications including *Dual Coast Magazine, Aardvark Press, Jitter Press, 50 Word Stories, Right Hand Pointing Press* and *Emerge Literary Journal*. Her work has also been recognized with a poetry award from the Lilian Osborn Memorial Foundation.

Nina Longfield resides in the Willamette Valley of western Oregon. In recent years, her writing delves the area between memory, place, and liminal space. Her poetry and short fiction has appeared in a variety of journals and anthologies. Please visit her at www.ninalongfield.com.

Penny Gibson lives in the beautiful Sherbrooke forest in Victoria, Australia where she writes poetry and short fiction.

Rasma Haidri grew up in Tennessee and currently lives on the arctic seacoast of Norway where she teaches British and American studies. Her poems and essays have been widely anthologized by publishers including P*uddinghouse, Seal Press, Bayeux Arts, Marion Street Press, The Chicago Review Press* and *Grayson Books*. *Literary journals featuring her work include Sycamore Review, Nimrod, Prairie Schooner, Passages North, Runes* and *The I-70 Review*. Her most recent work is forthcoming in *Veils, Halos and Shackles: International Poetry on the Abuse and Oppression of Women*, and *Songs for a Passbook Torch: Poems about Nelson Mandela*. Among her distinctions are the Southern Women Writers Association Emerging Writer Award in Creative Non-fiction, and the Wisconsin Academy of Arts, Letters & Science Poetry Award.

Farmer and poet **Robyn Sykes** writes, observes, works and learns on her family farm, surrounded by her inspiration. During her 30-plus years of rural life she has won two Henry Lawson awards; had stories, articles and poems published; edited the *Yass Tribune* and with her husband raised four sons.

Ron C. Moss is a visual artist and poet from Tasmania, Australia. His haiku and related genres have won many international prizes and he has been published in numerous journals and anthologies including, *Haiku in English: The First Hundred Years, W. W. Norton & Company* and *Where the River Goes: The Nature Tradition in English-Language Haiku*, Edited by Allan Burns, Snapshot Press.

Ron won the prestigious Seashell Game in 2011 for his haiku 'Starry Night.' Ron is a recipient of The Touchstone Awards for Individual Poems 2013 and The Touchstone Distinguished Books Award 2014 for his first collection, *The Bone Carver*, Snapshot Press. He is resident artist for the online journal, *A Hundred Gourds* and also the annual *Muttering Thunder*. Ron is well known for his haiga paintings, illustration and design, and is an award winning photographer. Email: ronmoss8@gmail.com Website: www.ronmoss.com

S. G. Larner lives in hot, humid Brisbane, where summer is unwelcome and winter eagerly anticipated by many residents. She has three children and is studying a Masters of Information Science. Her work has appeared in *Tincture Journal, Apex*, and more, and you can find her at http://foregoreality.wordpress.com.

S.E. Street's writing has been published in Australia and New Zealand as well as in the United States. She is recipient of The Dymocks Short Story Prize for fiction, the 2014 Hunter Writers Award and the 2014 SCWC HARP winner for poetry.

Sandra Simpson lives in Tauranga in New Zealand. She is *Haiku NewZ* website editor, South Pacific editor for the *Red Moon* anthologies, and secretary of the Katikati Haiku Pathway Committee. She has won several international awards for her haiku. Sandra is a programmer and publicist for the Tauranga Arts Festival, and is also a freelance journalist and editor.

Sarah Rice won the inaugural Ron Pretty Poetry Award, 2014 Bruce Dawe, co-won the 2011 Gwen Harwood, shortlisted in the 2013 Montreal, and Tom Howard poetry prizes. Publications include *Those Who Travel* (Ampersand Duck 2010), *Global Poetry Anthology, Award Winning Australian Writing, Best Australian Poetry, Island, Southerly, Australian Poetry Journal*.

SB Wright was born in the town of Nhulunbuy in Arnhem Land, though most of his life has been spent in Alice Springs. A graduate of NTU he has spent his adult working life as a security guard, a martial arts instructor, a trainer in an international gaming company and as a secondary school teacher. His work has been published in *Tincture Journal, INDaily Adelaide, Eureka Street, Bluepepper, A Hundred Gourds* and the anthologies *The Stars Like Sand* and *50 Haikus*.

Simon Hanson has been falling deeper into the spell of haiku for around six years now and imagines he has a long way to fall yet. He has learnt enough to realise that he shall always remain an apprentice to life and to nature that so inspire him. His haiku and related forms are regularly published in various Australian and international journals. He also has a collection of longer poetry, *Glowing in the Dark* - published by the Wakefield Press in 2011.

Stu Hatton is a poet, collagist, critic & editor based in Campbells Creek, Victoria. He has published two poetry collections: *How to be Hungry* (2010) and

Glitching (2014). He sometimes posts things at http://outerblog.tumblr.com.

Stuart Barnes was born in Hobart in 1977 and educated at Monash University. *The Staysails* (UQP, August 2016) won the 2015 Arts Queensland Thomas Shapcott Poetry Prize. Since 2013 he has been poetry editor for *Tincture Journal*. Visit him at his website https://stuartabarnes.wordpress.com/ and/or follow him on Twitter @StuartABarnes.

SuzAnne C. Cole, former college English instructor, writes in the Texas Hill Country. Both a juried and featured poet at the Houston Poetry Fest, she's also won a Japanese haiku contest. Her poetry and fiction have been nominated for a Pushcart Prize. She also writes essays and plays.

Tina Schumann's manuscript *As If* (Split Oak Press) was awarded the 2010 Stephen Dunn Poetry Prize. Her full manuscript was named a finalist in the Four Way Books Intro Prize and the National Poetry Series. She is the recipient of the American Poet Prize and a Pushcart nominee and a featured poet at the 2014 Skagit River Poetry Festival. Tina is the Assistant Director of Artsmith.org and editor of the forthcoming anthology, *Two-Countries: U.S. Daughters and Sons of Immigrant Parents*. Her poems have appeared widely, including *The American Poetry Journal, Ascent, Cimarron Review, Crab Creek Review, Midwest Quarterly, Nimrod, Palabra, Parabola, Poemeleon, Poetry International, Terrain.org* and the *Yale Journal for Humanities in Medicine*. To learn more about Tina please go to www.tinaschumann.com

Traudl Tan, a retired High School Teacher and member of WA Poets Inc, and Peter Cowan Writers Centre has poems published in the online poetry journal *Creatrix*.

Valentina Cano is a student of classical singing who spends whatever free time she has either reading or writing. Her works have appeared in numerous publications and her poetry has been nominated for the Pushcart Prize and Best of the Web. Her debut novel, *The Rose Master*, was published in 2014 and was called a "strong and satisfying effort" by Publishers Weekly.

Vanessa Proctor, besides writing free verse, has a special interest in haiku and its related forms, including renku. Her poetry long and short has been widely published internationally. In 2010 one of her haiku was inscribed on a boulder on the Katikati Haiku Pathway in New Zealand. Her latest publication is the eChapbook *Jacaranda Baby* (Snapshot Press, 2012).

Veronica Lake has been a Literature teacher in a Western Australian high school since the dawn of time. She was awarded a Churchill Fellow in 2010 for the teaching of Shakespeare. She produces and edits *Primo Lux* - an annual student poetry anthology. Her poems are published in several Australian journals.

Wes Lee lives in Wellington, New Zealand. Her chapbook *Cowboy Genes* was published by Grist Books at the University of Huddersfield in 2014. She was the 2010 recipient of The BNZ Katherine Mansfield Literary Award. Her poetry has recently appeared in *Westerly, Cordite, Poetry London, Magma, Landfall, Underneath: The University of Canberra Vice-Chancellor's Poetry Prize Anthology 2015*, and *The London Magazine*.

Publication Credits and Notes

What if I Knew of The Upstairs Lounge? (James Croteau) First published in a slightly different version in *The About Place Journal*. The UpStairs Lounge, a gay bar in New Orleans, was destroyed in an arson's fire on June 24, 1973. It was the deadliest fire in the city's history and the largest mass killing of LGBT people in the United States. The information about the fire and its aftermath is taken from news stories of the day and historical accounts.

paddy field, mountain mist (Billy Antonio) First published in *Asahi Shimbun*, September 19, 2014, *Akitsu Quarterly* Winter 2014.

blackberry winter (Elliot Nicely) First published in *Acorn* #33.

The Woodland Chapel (Jill Jones) First published in *Two Thirds North* (Sweden), March 2015.

Petasus' and Petal's Next (Joyce Parkes) Warming of the climate system is unequivocal as is now evident from observation of increases in global average air and ocean temperatures, widespread melting of snow and ice and rising global average sea levels. IPCC Climate Change 2007: Synthesis Report, p.72.

dreaming of childhood (Judit Katalin Hollos) First published in *Paper Wasp*, summer of 2015.

Heat, Flies and Cane Toads (S. G. Larner) First published in *Tincture Journal* #7.

Stoplight Outside Hamburger Harry's, 2:00 a.m. (Tina Schumann) First published in *San Pedro River Review*.

Now You Know it All Goes on Beyond You Don't You (Stu Hatton) A cento based on Matt Hetherington's book *Eye to Eye* (De-Repression Press, 2012).

Fingal (Stuart Barnes) First published in an earlier version in *Poetry Ireland Review*, 2011.

Brohmon (Journey) (Amelia Walker) First published in *Social Alternatives* vol. 30, no. 2, this version a reworked excerpt from a longer sequence.

Nullarbor at Night (Faith de Savigné) First published in *StoryMondo.com*.

The Flooded Field (Frances Donovan) First published in *Borderlands: Texas Poetry Review*.

Her Country (Gabrielle Rowe) First published in *ACU Poetry Prize Chapbook*.

Undersong (Irene Wilkie) first appeared in a short film released by the Kitchen Table Poets.

Dudgeon (jenni nixon) First published in *Seeking the Sun* – Central Coast Poets 2012.

An Afterlife of Stone (Jenny Blackford) First published in *A Slow Combusting Hymn*, August 2014.

Tabula Rasa (Les Wicks) First published in *Eureka St*.

Casglu Afalau / Apple Picking (Ivy Alvarez) First published in *Scintilla*, issue #16, 2013.

jellyfish at sea (Nichola Scholes) First published in *Under the Basho*, December 2015.

Tom Boy Poet (Nikki Carr) First published in *Emerge Literary Journal*, Issue 9, 2014.

Death in Nepal (SuzAnne C. Cole) First published in *Boiling River,* #1, 2/2009.

Crossing the Harbour Bridge (Vanessa Proctor) was Commended in the 2015 W.B Yeats Poetry Prize for Australia.

stargazing ... (Ron C. Moss) First published in *Yellow Moon* 15 (winter 2004).

Inland – haiku sequence (Lorin Ford)
The individual haiku in 'Inland' were first published (in order of appearance in the sequence) in (1) *paper wasp* 18.4; (2) 1st prize 2005 Shiki Salon Annual Haiku Awards; (3) *Presence* #49; (4)*The Heron's Nest* Volume XV :3; (5)*The Heron's Nest* Volume XVI:4; (6) *Presence* #49 and (7)*Shamrock Haiku Journal* # 5.

www.ingramcontent.com/pod-product-compliance
Lightning Source LLC
Chambersburg PA
CBHW020617300426
44113CB00007B/681